Azure Automation Using the ARM Model

An In-Depth Guide to Automation with Azure Resource Manager

Shijimol Ambi Karthikeyan

Apress®

Azure Automation Using the ARM Model

Shijimol Ambi Karthikeyan
Bangalore, Karnataka, India

ISBN-13 (pbk): 978-1-4842-3218-7   ISBN-13 (electronic): 978-1-4842-3219-4
https://doi.org/10.1007/978-1-4842-3219-4

Library of Congress Control Number: 2017959334

Cover image by Freepik (`www.freepik.com`).

Managing Director: Welmoed Spahr
Editorial Director: Todd Green
Acquisitions Editor: Nikhil Karkal
Development Editor: Matthew Moodie/Priyanka Mehta
Technical Reviewer: Pranab Mazumdar
Coordinating Editor: Prachi Mehta
Copy Editor: Sharon Wilkey

Distributed to the book trade worldwide by Springer Science + Business Media New York, 233 Spring Street, 6th Floor, New York, NY 10013. Phone 1-800-SPRINGER, fax (201) 348-4505, e-mail `orders-ny@springer-sbm.com`, or visit `www.springeronline.com`. Apress Media, LLC is a California LLC and the sole member (owner) is Springer Science + Business Media Finance Inc (SSBM Finance Inc). SSBM Finance Inc is a **Delaware** corporation.

For information on translations, please e-mail `rights@apress.com`, or visit `www.apress.com/rights-permissions`.

Apress titles may be purchased in bulk for academic, corporate, or promotional use. eBook versions and licenses are also available for most titles. For more information, reference our Print and eBook Bulk Sales web page at `www.apress.com/bulk-sales`.

Any source code or other supplementary material referenced by the author in this book is available to readers on GitHub via the book's product page, located at `www.apress.com/978-1-4842-3218-7`. For more detailed information, please visit `www.apress.com/source-code`.

Printed on acid-free paper

*Dedicated to my dearest Amma and Achan, my guardian angels
watching over me from heaven*

Contents at a Glance

Contents

About the Author

Shijimol A. K. currently works as a Partner Technical Consultant for Microsoft Partner Technical Services team. She has more than 11 years of experience in IT and specializes in datacenter management, virtualization, and cloud computing technologies. She started her career with EY IT services, on a datacenter management team managing complex virtualized production datacenters. She has expertise in managing VMware and Hyper-V virtualization stacks and Windows/Linux server technologies. She has also worked on DevOps CI/CD implementation projects using tools such as TeamCity, Jenkins, Git, TortoiseSVN, Mercurial, and Selenium. She later moved on to cloud computing and gained expertise in Windows Azure, focusing on Azure IaaS, Backup/DR, and Automation. She holds industry standard certifications in technologies including Microsoft Azure, Windows Server, and VMware. She also holds ITIL and TOGAF 9 certifications.

About the Technical Reviewer

Pranab Mazumdar is currently working as an embedded escalation engineer for Microsoft, focusing on Azure SQL Database (PaaS and IaaS) and Azure SQL Data Warehouse. He works closely with the engineering team to improve the service and make it a world-class stateful service, helping customers and partners be successful with their businesses. Prior to aligning to the cloud side of the business, he was an escalation engineer with the SQL Server team in CSS/GBS, where he worked with the product team to fix bugs in the SQL Server product, thereby making SQL a better and preferred RDBMS. He has been working with Microsoft for over 12 years, with specializations in SQL Server engine performance, high availability, and disaster recovery. He has worked with many large corporations on complex SQL deployments. Apart from SQL, he also has worked with Operational Insights, formerly known as System Center Advisor, migrating and helping create new sets of rules and validation processes. He holds several Microsoft certifications, including MCAD, MCSD, MCDBA, MSCE, MCTS, MCITP, and MCT; his most recent certification is Microsoft Certified Solutions Associate: Cloud Platform. He likes to be connected to his customers and has been a speaker at TechEd, GIDS, SQL Saturday, SQL Talks, and other community UG events. Recently, he coauthored *Pro SQL Server on Microsoft Azure* and was the technical reviewer of *Practical Azure Application Development*.

Acknowledgments

First and foremost, I would like to thank my parents for everything I have ever accomplished in my life, including this book. My mother, Ambi R., inspired me to aim for the stars. My father, Karthikeyan M., taught me to be patient while doing so. They are no longer around, but their love and blessings keep me going.

My husband, Sujai Sugathan, supported me throughout this new endeavor as he always does for all my adventures. He kept reminding me about the deadlines so that my editors didn't have to. My daughter, Sanjana Sujai, did her bit too by being the most wonderful and understanding seven-year-old. I am thankful to my sister, Gigimol A.K.; my mother-in-law, Sowja Sugathan; and my best friend, Anjana S; these strong women in my life always inspire me to take up new challenges. I am also thankful to the mentors in my professional life—there are too many to list—for their constant support and encouragement. Last but not least, I would like to thank the team at Apress: Nikhil Karkal for onboarding me, Prachi Mehta for her support during the publishing process, and Pranab Mazumdar and Priyanka Mehta for their valuable input during the review process.

Introduction

Microsoft Azure cloud adoption is on the rise, and Azure Automation plays a key role in building a sustainable and repeatable framework for creating and managing resources in Azure. This book will provide you an in-depth understanding of the options available in Azure Automation via the Azure Resource Manager (ARM) portal.

Microsoft recommends the ARM model as the way forward for all Azure deployments. This book focuses exclusively on the ARM deployment model for Azure Automation. This model has more robust options when compared to the classic deployment model.

This book provides in-depth coverage of topics such as runbook authoring and types of Automation runbooks. It also covers advanced topics including hybrid cloud automation from the ARM-based Azure portal.

Chapter 1, "Introduction to Azure Automation," introduces Azure Automation, providing an overview of features and guidelines on getting started with the service in the ARM portal.

Chapter 2, "Azure Automation Assets," explores the basic building blocks of runbooks, called *Automation assets*. These assets include schedules, modules, certificates, connections, variables, and credentials.

Chapter 3, "Azure Automation Runbook Types," covers the various runbook types in Azure Automation: PowerShell, PowerShell Workflow, Graphical and Graphical PowerShell Workflow. This chapter gives a walk-through of runbook creation, testing, and publishing.

Chapter 4, "Azure Automation DSC," covers integration of Azure Automation with PowerShell Desired State Configuration(DSC), including various cloud, on-premises, and hybrid scenarios.

Chapter 5, "Hybrid Cloud Automation," covers the Hybrid Runbook Worker in Azure Automation, which facilitates execution of runbooks in your on-premises datacenters or systems hosted in third-party cloud service providers.

Chapter 6, "Sample Runbooks and Use Cases," provides a walk-through of some popular use cases and their implementations using Azure Automation.

This book is written for infrastructure and cloud architects, cloud support engineers, system administrators, and IT strategists with a basic understanding of the Azure cloud platform and PowerShell scripting.

CHAPTER 1

■ ■ ■

Introduction to Azure Automation

Automating operational tasks is critical for streamlining infrastructure management, both on premises and in the cloud. Microsoft Azure Automation comes with capabilities that help administrators automate their cloud-based, operational, repetitive tasks. It is versatile, with hybrid connection capabilities that help you automate tasks in your on-premises datacenters as well as with other cloud service providers like Amazon Web Services (AWS). Being built on top of the ever-reliable PowerShell, it is a useful tool in the arsenal of any Azure cloud administrator. Azure runbooks are easy to create, edit, and execute and can integrate well with almost all resources in the Microsoft Azure ecosystem.

Azure Automation has significantly changed since its inception as a small feature in the Azure classic portal. With the introduction of the Azure Resource Manager (ARM) model and the new Azure portal, Azure Automation also significantly ramped up, with many new features such as Azure Graphical runbooks. As more and more organizations are moving toward the cloud, automation is also much in demand to maximize the return on investment (ROI). Microsoft Azure is a leader in the cloud market, and developing skillsets in Azure Automation is a valuable tool in the arsenal of a cloud administrator.

This chapter introduces you to the ARM deployment model in Azure and the various components of Azure Automation in the ARM model. These include but are not limited to the Azure Automation overview dashboard, PowerShell, runbooks, jobs, Runbook Gallery, hybrid workers, and Azure Automation security. We will focus on establishing a basic understanding of the key concepts of Azure Automation, which will be explained in detail in subsequent chapters.

■ **Note** Azure has two deployment models: the classic, or Azure Service Management (ASM), model and the more recent Azure Resource Manager (ARM) model. This book focuses on the ARM deployment model.

© Shijimol Ambi Karthikeyan 2017
S. Ambi Karthikeyan, *Azure Automation Using the ARM Model*,
https://doi.org/10.1007/978-1-4842-3219-4_1

Azure ARM Deployment Model

The ARM model is the way forward for all Azure deployments as recommended by Microsoft. Compared to the monolithic deployment model of the Azure classic portal, ARM brings in flexibility and robustness with features including resource groups, role-based access control, template deployments, tagging, and resource policy. Let's look at some of the key features of the ARM model before delving into Azure Automation, because many of these features will prominently feature in some of the Automation runbooks that we will be discussing further in this book.

RBAC

Azure role-based access control (RBAC) helps you implement fine-grained access restrictions on resources created in Azure. In the classic model, there was only one role, named *Co-administration*, which had full access to the entire Azure subscription. This was not suitable when administrators wanted to implement more restrictions at at the resource level. With the introduction of RBAC, there are many predefined roles that you can leverage.

In addition, you can even create your own roles. The three main roles are Reader, Contributor, and Owner. You can apply the roles at various scopes—to resource groups, virtual machines (VMs), or networks, for example.. The Owner role has full permission to the applied scope and enables the member of the role to add another user in the given scope. The Contributor role also has full access, but a member of the Contributor group cannot add another user to the scope. Reader provides only read access to any applied scope. In addition, each resource type has its own set of predefined roles that an administrator can leverage to set permissions.

Template Deployment

In the ARM model, you have the option to automate the deployment of resources by using JSON templates. This is useful for deploying complex multitier environments in a single click. You can define the parameters in JSON format, define dependencies, and then create a template for complex architectures. This is useful in crash-and-burn scenarios and time-sensitive deployments.

Tags

You can tag the resources in Azure with a key/value pair so that you can do a logical marking of resources coming under a certain scope. For example, you can create a tag for all development resources in your environment, and when you select the tag from the portal, Azure will list all the resources coming under that tag. Tags are also useful for billing purposes. In the Azure consumption bill, you can filter resources based on their tags. This will help you identify the cost incurred by a resource grouped under a given tag. One possible use case is cross-charging; you can create a tag for all resources for another department, sort the charges based on the tag, and cross-charge to a respective department.

Resource Groups

Azure resource groups are a new feature in ARM that enable you to logically group related resources and manage them as a single entity. Any resource created in the ARM model should be part of a resource group, and it can be part of only one resource group at a given time. Adding resources to a resource group allows you to manage their life cycle and create a security boundary. Grouping resources in resource groups becomes relevant when you want to be able to create, update, or delete them together.

Resource Policies

Resource policies allow administrators to implement restrictions in terms of resource locations or naming conventions. A policy consists of a policy definition and policy assignment at a given scope. Resource policies are quite useful when cloud administrators want to implement certain rules and regulations—for example, all created resources should reside in a chosen Azure location, or the resources should adhere to a given naming convention. Unlike RBAC, which decides the permission levels of a user at a given scope, policies define the properties of the resources at the applied scope, such as their naming conventions or location.

Azure Automation in the ARM Portal

The concept of cloud computing is heavily dependent on automation, wherein users can log in and spin up resources based on their requirements. More and more organizations are adopting the cloud-first policy, and hence there is an increasing demand on automating long-running complex operational tasks in the cloud. Azure Automation was introduced to fill this gap.

Automation was introduced in the classic portal initially. With the introduction of the ARM model and the strategy of promoting it for all services new and old, Automation was introduced in the ARM-based portal as well. The new ARM-based portal is simply referred to as the *Azure portal*. Automation runbooks are based on PowerShell and bring in the exciting possibilities of PowerShell scripting to the Azure platform in an easy-to-handle interface.

Creating Your Automation Account and Getting Started

Let's look at how to create an automation account in the ARM portal:

1. Go to the Azure portal. In the left panel, click More Services and then type in **automation** (Figure 1-1).

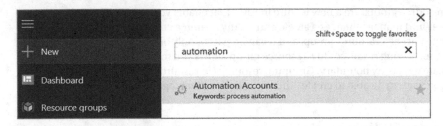

Figure 1-1. *Searching with the automation keyword*

2. A list of automation accounts is displayed. To create a new account, click Add (Figure 1-2).

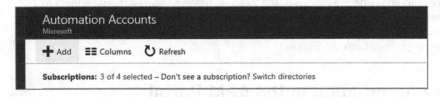

Figure 1-2. *Adding a new Automation account*

3. You need to provide some information while creating the Automation account (Figure 1-3). The Automation account should have a unique name and be assigned to a resource group. You can either use an existing resource group or create a new resource group.

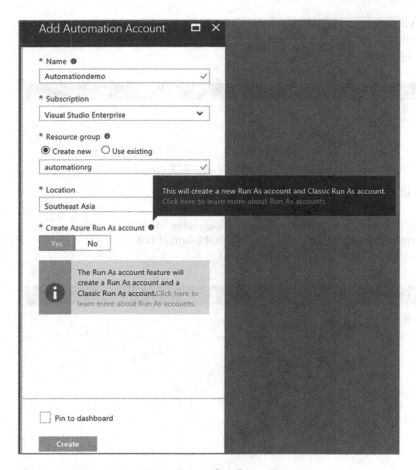

Figure 1-3. *New Automation account details*

4. You also have an option to create a new Run As account in the classic (a.k.a. Service Management) as well as the Azure portal. Run As accounts are required to authenticate with Azure to create and manage resources using your runbooks. In the case of ARM, the account that gets created is a service principal in Azure Active Directory, along with an associated certificate. This account gets the Contributor role by default. The classic Run As account that gets created uses the concept of certificate authentication in the Service Management model. It uploads a management certificate that can be used to access and manage classic portal resources by the Automation runbooks. The classic portal is being deprecated and is beyond the scope of this book.

5. When you click the Create button, the Automation account is created. It is then listed under the Automation accounts in the Azure portal (Figure 1-4).

Figure 1-4. *Automation account list*

6. If you click the Automation account, Azure takes you to the overview, which provides a nice tiled dashboard of various components included in it (Figure 1-5).

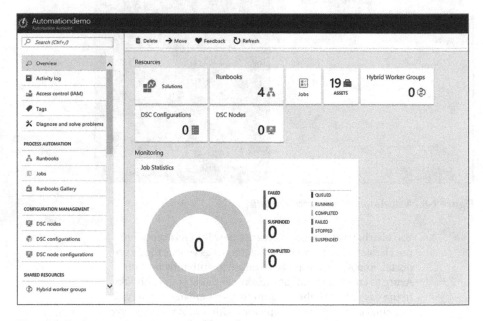

Figure 1-5. *Automation account dashboard*

Exploring the Dashboard

We will be discussing many of these components in detail in this book, and we'll start off with a brief introduction to them now.

Solutions

Automation accounts can be linked with the Operations Management Suite (OMS), and the solutions connected to it (Figure 1-6).

Figure 1-6. OMS Solutions list

You can integrate your automation account directly with OMS. Alternately, you can create webhooks for runbooks and execute them based on OMS search criteria. This is explained in detail in Chapter 5, Hybrid Cloud Automation.

Runbooks

Runbooks are the basic building blocks of Azure Automation. You can create your own runbooks for various tasks to be executed via the Automation platform. A Runbook Gallery is available that has many runbooks already published by Microsoft or community contributors; you can import these runbooks, customize them, and schedule them based on your requirements (Figure 1-7).

Runbooks

➕ Add a runbook   📖 Browse gallery   ↻ Refresh

🔍 |

	NAME	AUTHORING STATUS	LAST MODIFIED	TA
⛭	AzureAutomationTutorial	✔ Published	2/21/2017 7:28 AM	
⅀	AzureAutomationTutorialScript	✔ Published	2/21/2017 3:12 PM	
⛭	AzureClassicAutomationTutorial	✔ Published	2/21/2017 7:28 AM	
⅀	AzureClassicAutomationTutorial...	✔ Published	2/21/2017 7:28 AM	
⛭	StartAzureV2Vm1	✔ Published	3/7/2017 11:43 AM	
⛭	StopAzureV2Vm	✏ In edit	2/27/2017 9:35 AM	
⅀	testpowershell	✏ In edit	2/27/2017 9:36 AM	

Figure 1-7. *List of runbooks*

Jobs

The Jobs panel in the overview gives information about runbook execution status. You can drill down deeper and get information on the input, output, and more. Each time a runbook execution is initiated, either via a schedule or manually, a job is created. An Azure automation worker executes the job. Many jobs can run in parallel; one runbook might have multiple jobs being executed. You can also view the job status in the dashboard (Figure 1-8).

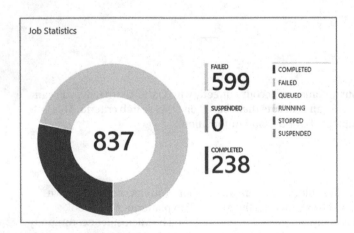

Figure 1-8. *Job Statistics overview*

Multiple statuses can be associated with a job. These include Completed, Failed, Queued, Running, Stopped, and Suspended:

Completed: Indicates that the job execution completed successfully.

Failed: The job failed to execute. It could be because of compilation errors or execution errors based on the runbook type.

Queued: The Azure Automation worker is not available to execute the job, and hence it is in a queue.

Running: The job is being executed.

Stopped: This indicates that the user stopped the job execution while it was running.

Suspended: The job is in a suspended state, for various possible reasons. It could be suspended manually by a user or by a command in the script. A user can restart the runbook at any given time, and it will restart from the beginning if there are no checkpoints in the script.

Assets

Assets in an Automation account consist of the following components: schedules, modules, certificates, connections, variables, and credentials (Figure 1-9). Azure Automation assets are discussed in detail in Chapter 2.

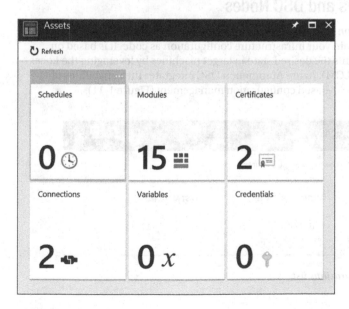

Figure 1-9. *Assets overview*

Hybrid Worker Groups

You can use Azure Automation to execute runbooks in your on-premises environment as well. You need to deploy Azure automation hybrid workers to on-premises servers and connect them to your Azure Automation account. You can get a list of such hybrid workers from the overview dashboard (Figure 1-10).

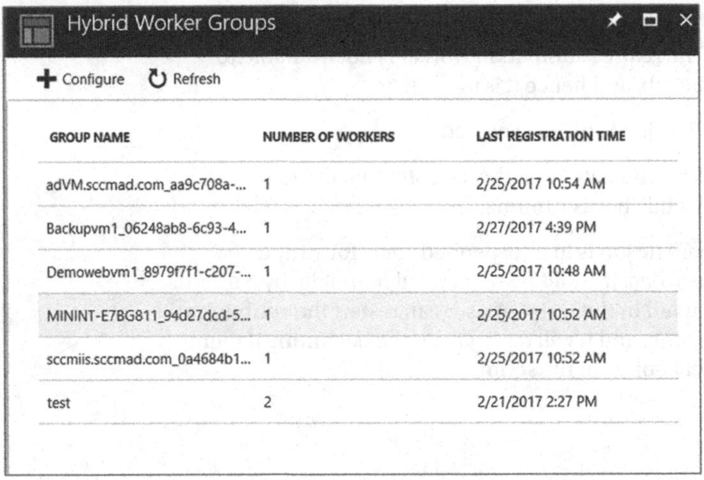

Figure 1-10. List of Hybrid Worker Groups

DSC Configurations and DSC Nodes

Desired State Configuration (DSC), as the name indicates, is a configuration management solution that helps maintain your infrastructure configuration as code. It is based on PowerShell and implements the desired state in target machines by leveraging the Local Configuration Manager (LCM). Azure Automation DSC integrates the capabilities of Azure Automation with DSC-based configuration management (Figure 1-11).

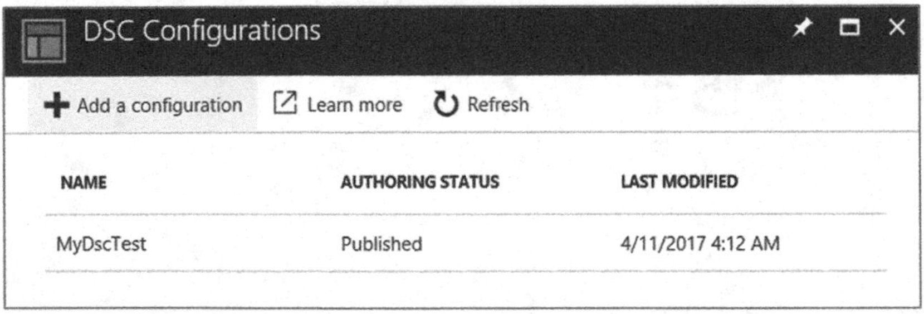

Figure 1-11. DSC configurations list

10

By leveraging Azure Automation DSC, you can manage the desired state of your infrastructure configuration across on-premises physical/virtual machines as well as cloud resources. We will discuss Azure Automation DSC configuration in detail later in this book in Chaper 4.

PowerShell in Azure Automation

The runbooks in Azure automation are completely based on PowerShell. Four types of runbooks are available: PowerShell, PowerShell Workflow, Graphical, and Graphical PowerShell Workflow. Though based on PowerShell, each runbook type has its own features and limitations.

PowerShell

These are the basic PowerShell-based runbooks available in Azure Automation. Using these runbooks is similar to executing Azure PowerShell module-based commands from the Azure portal. The related PowerShell modules should already be imported in your Azure Automation account.

Certain capabilities such as parallel processing of tasks and runbook checkpoints are not available in these basic PowerShell-based runbooks. You will have to go for PowerShell Workflow–based runbooks if you want to use these features. You can create runbooks by using the simple Azure PowerShell-based scripts that you might be already using to manage your Azure infrastructure, and leverage additional capabilities such as scheduling them.

PowerShell Workflow

PowerShell Workflow runbooks are intended for more-complex tasks that involve executing steps in parallel, calling other child runbooks, and so forth. As the name indicates, this type of runbook is written using PowerShell workflows that in turn use Windows Workflow Foundation. PowerShell workflows allow you to set checkpoints in your script so that you can restart the script from the checkpoint if an exception occurs during execution. This kind of workflow can cater to advanced automation requirements of complex cloud infrastructures.

Graphical

Graphical runbooks can be created from the Azure portal, but unlike the PowerShell and PowerShell Workflow runbooks, they cannot be edited or created outside the portal. They use PowerShell in the back end, but the process is transparent to the user. There is an option to convert the Graphical runbooks to Graphical PowerShell Workflow, and vice versa.

Graphical runbooks are a good place to start for a cloud administrator who doesn't have much expertise in PowerShell. This type of runbook uses a visual authoring model and represents the data flow pictorially in an easy-to-understand fashion. The editing can also be done directly from the portal, against each building block of the runbook, to implement changes in the logic.

Graphical PowerShell Workflow

Graphical PowerShell Workflow runbooks are based on PowerShell workflows in the back end. Other than that, the properties are the same as that of a Graphical runbook. Graphical PowerShell Workflow runbooks can be edited and managed only from within the Azure portal.

Runbook Gallery

A Runbook Gallery is readily available in the Azure portal, where several runbooks catering to multiple scenarios are already available. Some of these runbooks are contributed by the community, and others are provided by Microsoft. You can access the Runbook Gallery by clicking the runbook tiles in the overview dashboard of the Automation account.

Click Overview ➤ Runbooks ➤ Browse Gallery to access the gallery (Figure 1-12).

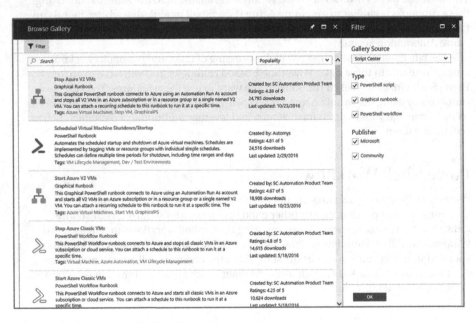

Figure 1-12. *Azure Runbook Gallery*

On the right-hand side, you can see the Gallery Source listed. It could be either Script Center (which is the default) or the PowerShell Gallery. You will find scripts/runbooks more relevant to Azure by choosing the Script Center option. The PowerShell Gallery contains mostly general-purpose PowerShell scripts. This right-hand pane also provides an option to filter the runbooks based on their type (PowerShell Script, Graphical Runbook, or PowerShell Workflow). Further filtering is possible based on the publisher (you can choose runbooks published by Microsoft or by the community).

You can search for runbooks for specific use cases in the search bar. Usually, runbooks are readily available for all major Automation use cases. If not, you will find something close enough that you can tweak and reuse.

Select the runbook from the gallery, and you can review the information about the runbook from its description. For Graphical runbooks, you can review the dataflow in a flow chart representation. You can import the runbook to your Automation account by clicking Import (Figure 1-13).

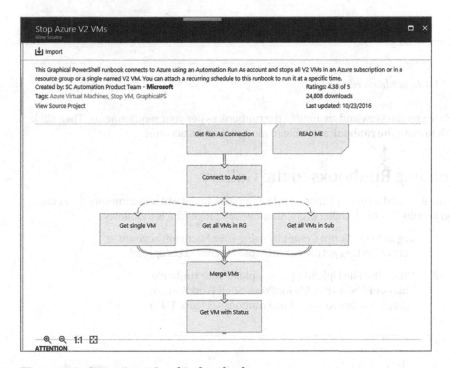

Figure 1-13. *Importing a Graphical runbook*

You need to provide a name and may provide an optional description while importing the runbook by using the Import option available in the portal). Once imported, the runbook will be listed in your Automation account. However, this runbook is not available for execution unless you publish it.

To publish the runbook, click Edit. This opens the runbook edit pane (Figure 1-14).

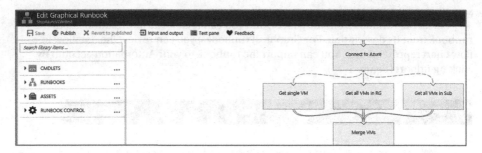

Figure 1-14. *Runbook edit pane*

Here you can view and customize the runbook as per your requirements. Then click Publish to make the runbook available in the Automation account.

Uploading Runbooks to the Gallery

If you have created a runbook that could be valuable to the wider community, you can upload it to the Runbook Gallery. The step-by-step procedure is as follows:

1. Log in to the Script Center by using your Microsoft account at `http://gallery.technet.microsoft.com/site/upload`.

2. Under the File Upload option, upload your runbooks. This could be a `.ps1` file for PowerShell Workflows or `.graphrunbook` for Graphical runbooks (Figure 1-15).

Figure 1-15. *File upload option*

3. Provide the title and description of your runbook (Figure 1-16).

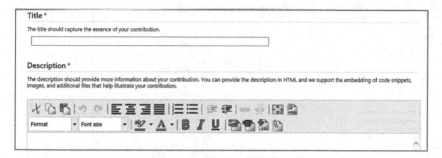

Figure 1-16. *Runbook title and description*

> You should list all dependencies of the runbook in the description. If runbooks refer to other runbooks, that information must be provided in the description, and the corresponding runbooks should have the same tag.

4. Provide a summary of the runbook and the language of choice (Figure 1-17). The summary will be displayed in the Runbook Gallery search results.

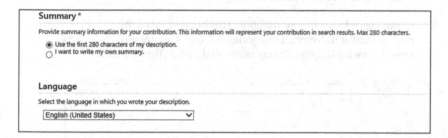

Figure 1-17. *Runbook summary*

5. In the next section, select the category as Windows Azure and the subcategory as Automation (Figure 1-18). The next option, operating system, is irrelevant in this case and can be ignored.

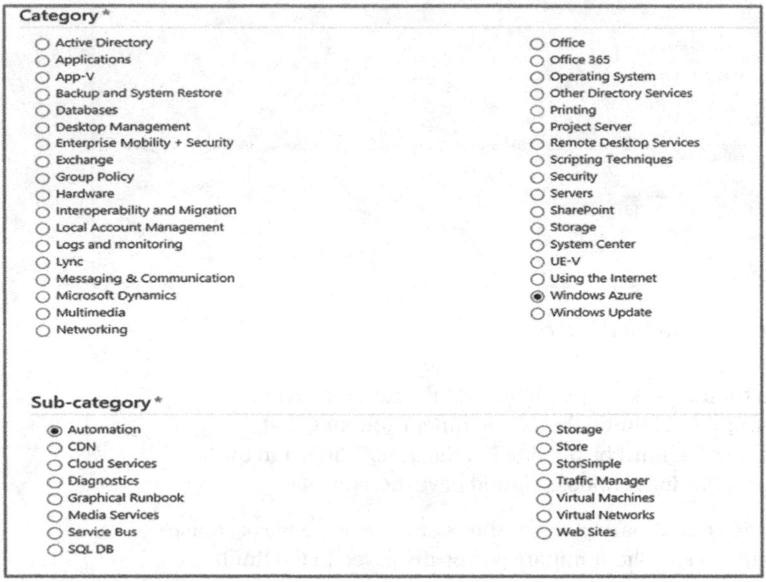

Category*

○ Active Directory
○ Applications
○ App-V
○ Backup and System Restore
○ Databases
○ Desktop Management
○ Enterprise Mobility + Security
○ Exchange
○ Group Policy
○ Hardware
○ Interoperability and Migration
○ Local Account Management
○ Logs and monitoring
○ Lync
○ Messaging & Communication
○ Microsoft Dynamics
○ Multimedia
○ Networking

○ Office
○ Office 365
○ Operating System
○ Other Directory Services
○ Printing
○ Project Server
○ Remote Desktop Services
○ Scripting Techniques
○ Security
○ Servers
○ SharePoint
○ Storage
○ System Center
○ UE-V
○ Using the Internet
◉ Windows Azure
○ Windows Update

Sub-category*

◉ Automation
○ CDN
○ Cloud Services
○ Diagnostics
○ Graphical Runbook
○ Media Services
○ Service Bus
○ SQL DB

○ Storage
○ Store
○ StorSimple
○ Traffic Manager
○ Virtual Machines
○ Virtual Networks
○ Web Sites

Figure 1-18. *Selecting the Category and Sub-category*

6. Assign tags relevant to your runbook. This helps in listing the runbook under the relevant categories. A Graphical runbook should have the GraphicalPS tag associated with it (Figure 1-19).

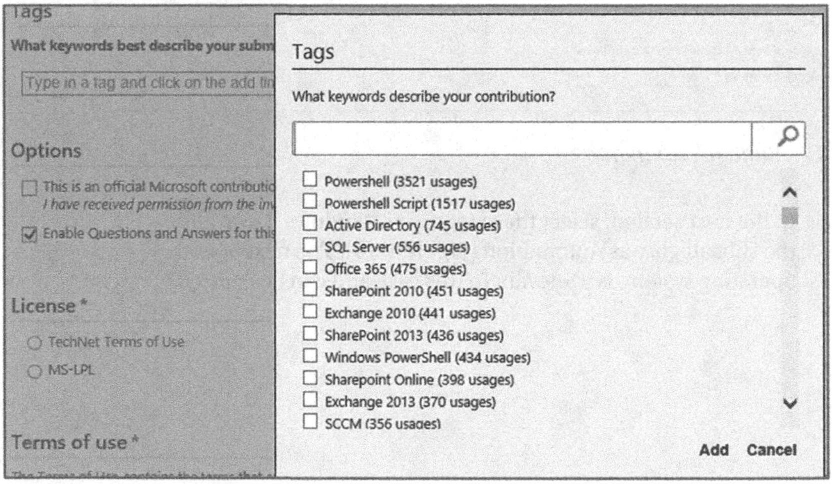

Tags

What keywords best describe your subm

Type in a tag and click on the add ti

Options

☐ This is an official Microsoft contributio
I have received permission from the in

☑ Enable Questions and Answers for this

License*

○ TechNet Terms of Use

○ MS-LPL

Terms of use*

Tags
_____

What keywords describe your contribution?

[   ] 🔍

☐ Powershell (3521 usages)   ∧
☐ Powershell Script (1517 usages)   ▪
☐ Active Directory (745 usages)
☐ SQL Server (556 usages)
☐ Office 365 (475 usages)
☐ SharePoint 2010 (451 usages)
☐ Exchange 2010 (441 usages)
☐ SharePoint 2013 (436 usages)
☐ Windows PowerShell (434 usages)
☐ Sharepoint Online (398 usages)
☐ Exchange 2013 (370 usages)   ∨
☐ SCCM (356 usages)

                              Add   Cancel

Figure 1-19. *Assigning tags*

7. You have the option to enable Q & A for this contribution or mark the runbook as an official Microsoft contribution if you have received permissions to do so (Figure 1-20).

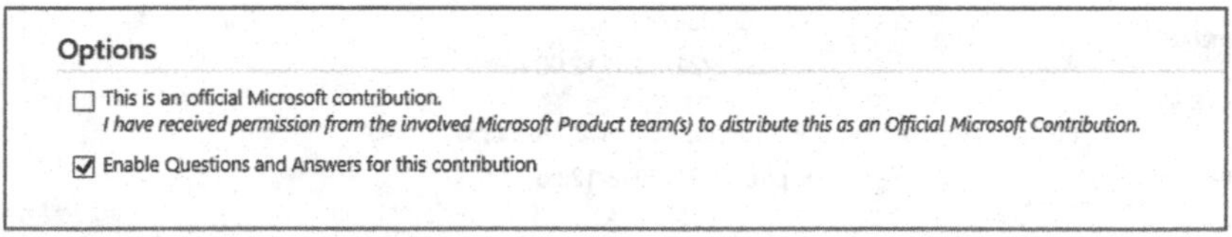

Options

☐ This is an official Microsoft contribution.
I have received permission from the involved Microsoft Product team(s) to distribute this as an Official Microsoft Contribution.

☑ Enable Questions and Answers for this contribution

Figure 1-20. *Enabling Q & A*

8. Select the License options: TechNet Terms of Use, MIT, or MS-LPL (Figure 1-21). TechNet terms of use refers to Microsoft Developer Services Agreement. MIT and MS-LPL come under open source licensing. The last step is to agree to the terms of use and submit the runbook.

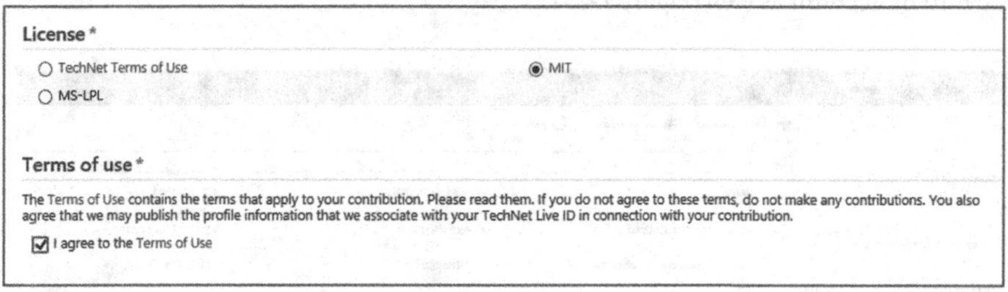

License *

○ TechNet Terms of Use   ◉ MIT
○ MS-LPL

Terms of use *

The Terms of Use contains the terms that apply to your contribution. Please read them. If you do not agree to these terms, do not make any contributions. You also agree that we may publish the profile information that we associate with your TechNet Live ID in connection with your contribution.

☑ I agree to the Terms of Use

Figure 1-21. *License options*

Azure Automation Security

Azure Automation should be linked with an Azure Automation account that has access to resources in the associated Azure subscription. In the classic model, certificate-based authentication was used. However, in the ARM model, Azure AD-based authentication is used. This simplifies the authentication process, as one account can be used for authenticating for both the classic and ARM models.

When you create the Automation account, Azure automatically creates a Run As account for both the ARM and classic models with the required permissions, as explained earlier. You can see the details of these accounts by selecting the Run As accounts from the respective Automation dashboard (Figure 1-22).

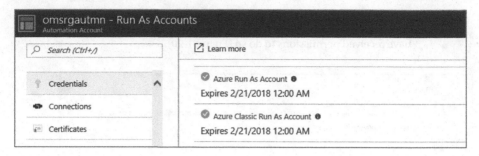

Figure 1-22. *Azure Automation Run As accounts*

You can click each account to view further details.

When the Azure Run As accounts are created, a couple of other resources are also created in the back end for the users to start with. These include two sample runbooks: one PowerShell-based runbook called `AzureAutomationTutorialScript`, and one Graphical runbook called `AzureAutomationTutorial`. These runbooks demonstrate how to authenticate by using the Run As accounts. Similarly, two runbooks are created for the classic Run As account as well (Figure 1-23).

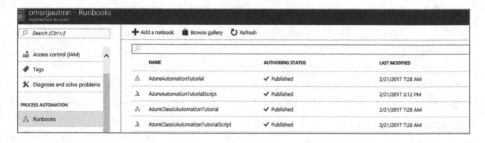

Figure 1-23. *Sample runbooks*

Click any of the runbooks and execute them to verify the Run As accounts

Let's start the `AzureAutomationTutorial` runbook to verify the ARM Run As accounts. Click the runbook, which takes you to the execution pane. Now click Start.

In the Job pane, click Output, and you should be able to view the output of the runbook , which is the list of all resources in your subscription (Figure 1-24).

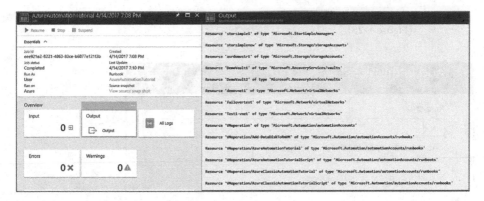

Figure 1-24. Sample Runbook output

You can repeat the same with `AzureClassicAutomationTutorial` to get similar results.

Role-Based Access Control

If you want to provide role-based access for different users to your Automation account, use the basic RBAC model of ARM. Along with the Owner, Contributor and Reader role, you can also use the Automation Operator role that is tailor made for Automation. In addition to these Four roles, you can also use the User Access Administrator role that can be assigned to manage user access to your Azure resources.

The Contributor role provides full read/write/delete permissions in the Automation account, except for providing another user access to the Automation resources. Reader, on the other hand, provides only read-level permissions, as the name indicates. The Automation Operator role, provides restrictive permissions to the assigned user. This role is specifically targeting users who need permissions to start, stop, suspend, or resume Azure Automation jobs and nothing else. It is useful when you want to provide delegated permissions to a team member to manage Azure Automation jobs.

Follow these steps to provide role-based access to a user:

1. Go to the Automation account and click Access Control (IAM), as shown in Figure 1-25.

Figure 1-25. Azure Automation access control (IAM)

2. Click the Add option. This opens the permissions pane (Figure 1-26).

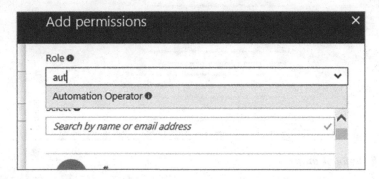

Figure 1-26. *Setting permissions*

Here you can search for the specific role and the username by name or email ID. The user should already be present in your Azure AD associated with the subscription. You can save the permission after you have added the user.

However, if you are using hybrid workers to execute runbooks against your on-premises datacenter, you should provide a credential with permissions to execute the runbook against the target machine. This is applicable for executing runbooks against AWS resources as well.

Let's look at how to add resources for hybrid workers. This involves creating a credential asset with the username/password.

3. From the Azure Automation dashboard, click Assets ➤ Credentials to open the Credentials dialog box (Figure 1-27).

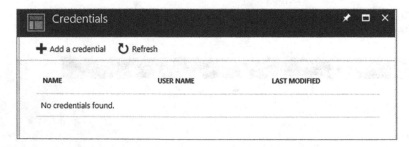

Figure 1-27. *Adding credentials*

4. Click the Add a Credential option and then provide the name, description, username, and password (Figure 1-28).

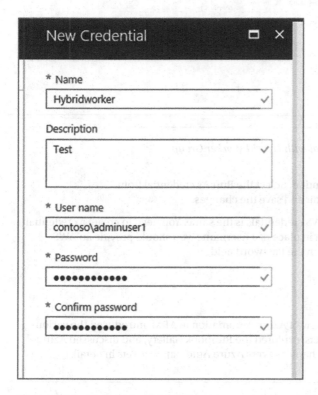

Figure 1-28. *New credential details*

The username in this case can be in the form of *domain\username* (as shown in Figure 1-28), *username@domain*, or simply the username alone if it is a local account.

You can call this credential in your runbooks, or alternately specify a Run As account for a given Hybrid Worker Group. That way, the credential is automatically invoked for authentication each time you execute a runbook against a Hybrid Worker Group.

5. To associate the credential with a Hybrid Worker Group, click the Hybrid Worker Group from the Automation dashboard. Select the target group and then click Hybrid Worker Group Settings (Figure 1-29).

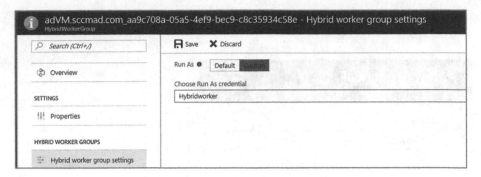

Figure 1-29. Associate credential with Hybrid Worker Group

6. Click the Custom option. Select the Run As credential from the drop-down menu and save the changes.

The process for creating AWS credentials is the same. You need to create a credential asset. The only difference is that in place of a username, you should provide an AWS access ID and secret access key in the Password field.

Summary

This chapter provided an overview of Azure Automation in ARM, introduced the various types of runbooks and their assets, explored the Runbook Gallery, and discussed Azure Automation security. The next chapter covers Azure Automation assets in detail.

■ Additional Resources

https://docs.microsoft.com/en-us/azure/automation/automation-intro

https://docs.microsoft.com/en-us/azure/automation/automation-runbook-types#graphical-runbooks

https://docs.microsoft.com/en-us/azure/automation/automation-offering-get-started

https://docs.microsoft.com/en-us/azure/automation/automation-runbook-gallery

https://docs.microsoft.com/en-us/azure/automation/automation-role-based-access-control

https://docs.microsoft.com/en-us/azure/automation/automation-hybrid-runbook-worker

https://docs.microsoft.com/en-us/azure/automation/automation-runbook-types

https://docs.microsoft.com/en-us/azure/automation/automation-runbook-types#powershell-runbooks

CHAPTER 2

■ ■ ■

Azure Automation Assets

This chapter covers the various Azure Automation assets and their relevance in Azure Automation. We will also look at nested runbooks, which enable modularity and reusability of runbooks. Automation assets play an important role in Azure Automation, as you can reference the assets within a runbook, and they will be accessed at different stages during runbook execution. Automation assets provide flexibility to the administrator since they can be defined once and reused whenever required. For example, you can create a schedule for repetitive execution of runbooks, and the same schedule can be linked to multiple runbooks. You can create a connection asset to establish connections to target resources, and this asset can be used by multiple runbooks. This chapter will give you a detailed understanding of Azure Automation assets and how they can be defined and leveraged in Azure Automation.

Azure Automation Assets

Assets in an Automation account can be considered globally available settings that can be used by runbooks in that given account. The assets are classified as schedules, modules, variables, connections, certificates, and credentials.

Schedules

One of the most important requirements of any automation framework is the capability to schedule repeated tasks. In Azure Automation, this is achieved by using the *schedules* asset. You can create schedules and attach them to runbooks so the runbooks are run repeatedly—on a daily, weekly, or monthly basis, for example. You can attach multiple runbooks to a schedule, and attach multiple schedules to a runbook.

© Shijimol Ambi Karthikeyan 2017
S. Ambi Karthikeyan, *Azure Automation Using the ARM Model*,
https://doi.org/10.1007/978-1-4842-3219-4_2

To create and attach a schedule to a runbook, follow these steps:

Click the Automation dashboard and then choose Assets ➤ Schedules. Next click on Add a Schedule (Figure 2-1).

Figure 2-1. *Azure Automation schedules*

Provide the information shown in Figure 2-2.

Figure 2-2. *Describing a new schedule*

In particular, you need to provide the following details:

- A name for the schedule

- Description

- A start time for the schedule, along with the time zone

- The recurrence is set to Once by default. However, you can set it to Recurring and configure the frequency as every Hour, Day, Week, or Month.

- By default, the expiration is set as No (the schedule never expires). However, you can set an expiry date and time for the schedule if required.

The next step is to link this schedule with a runbook. Open the target runbook. In the overview tab, select Schedules (Figure 2-3).

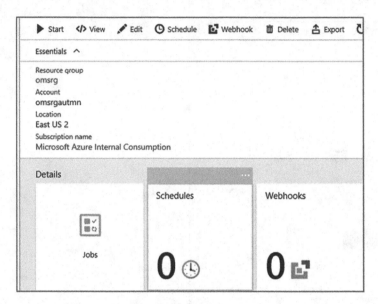

Figure 2-3. *Schedules in the overview tab*

Click the Add a Schedule option. Then link the schedule to your runbook and select the schedule (Figure 2-4).

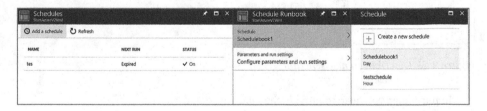

Figure 2-4. *Linking a schedule*

You can set the input parameters of the runbooks to be used for the schedule. In this example, the runbook input parameters include the resource group name (optional), the name of the VM(optional), and the connection asset name (which, if not provided, will use the default AzureRunAsConnector asset). You should also specify the run settings, which determine where the runbook gets executed (either on Azure or on a hybrid worker (Figure 2-5).

Figure 2-5. *Input parameters for the runbook*

If you wish to unlink the schedule from a runbook at any given point, you can select the schedule and then choose More ➤ Unlink (Figure 2-6).

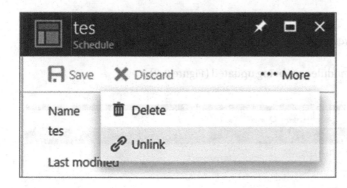

Figure 2-6. *Unlinking a schedule*

Modules

For the runbooks to be executed without any errors, the PowerShell *modules* corresponding to the commands being used should be imported into the Automation account. This concept is like that in standard PowerShell, where the respective modules should be made available in the PowerShell runtime before executing a PowerShell command. Like Runbook Gallery, a PowerShell Module Gallery is available in the Azure portal (Figure 2-7).

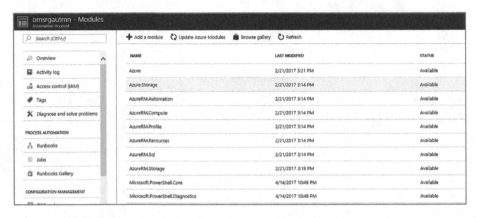

***Figure 2-7.** PowerShell module list*

The majority of the required PowerShell modules are readily available in the account by default. The Azure team regularly updates the modules. You can keep the modules in your account up-to-date by clicking Update Azure Modules.

You will then get a notification that all modules will be updated to the latest version. Click Yes (Figure 2-8).

***Figure 2-8.** Module update notification*

You can see that the modules are being updated (Figure 2-9).

***Figure 2-9.** Azure modules being updated*

Once the update is complete, you will be notified that the modules have been updated (Figure 2-10).

Figure 2-10. *Notification of update completion*

It is recommended to link and unlink any runbook schedules by using these modules, and to link them back after the modules are updated.

If any particular module is not available in the gallery, you can browse the PowerShell Gallery, search for the module, and import it. Click the Browse Gallery option to access the gallery, shown in Figure 2-11.

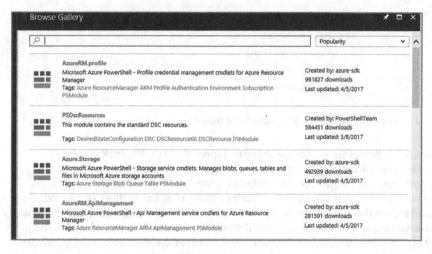

Figure 2-11. *Azure Automation module gallery*

Select the module that you would like to import to view the details, shown in Figure 2-12.

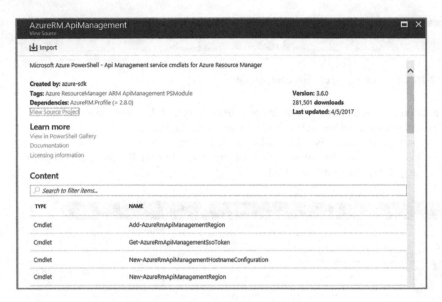

Figure 2-12. *Viewing the details of a PowerShell module*

In the preceding example, we are trying to import the AzureRM.ApiManagement module. This module contains Azure Storage management commands such as Add-AzureRmApiManagementRegion,Get-AzureRmApiManagementRegion, and New-AzureRmA piManagementHostnameConfiguration. If your runbook uses any of these commands, you should import this module to the Automation account before executing the runbook. Otherwise, you might get a Command Not Found error. Some of the modules will have a dependency on other modules. In this case, the AzureStorage module has a dependency on the AzureRM.Profile(=2.8.0) module. Therefore, the module should be imported and available in the account, and the version should be 2.8.0.

Click the Import option to import the module to your account (Figure 2-13).

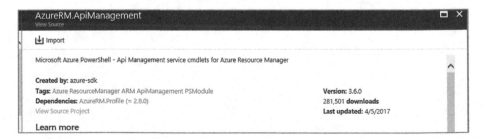

Figure 2-13. *Importing dependent modules*

You will get a message stating that importing a module might take couple of minutes. You will also see warning for any dependencies that need to be updated. You can choose to update the dependent modules when you import the new module (Figure 2-14).

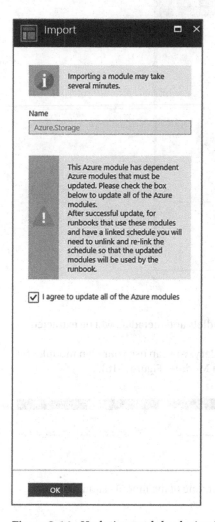

Figure 2-14. *Updating modules during import*

Click the OK button to proceed.
The progress of the import will be displayed in the portal (Figure 2-15).

Figure 2-15. Module update in progress

During the import process, the PowerShell cmdlets and metadata will be extracted and made available in the Automation account.

In addition to importing modules from the gallery, you can use your own modules by clicking Automation Accounts ➤ Modules ➤ Add a Module (Figure 2-16).

Figure 2-16. Importing a new Automation module

The module can be uploaded as a zip file. The name of the module should be the same as the zip file (Figure 2-17).

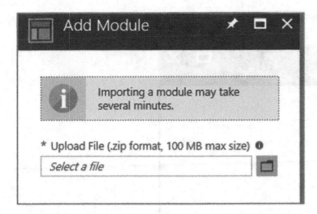

Figure 2-17. Uploading a module as a zip file

Variables

Variables are, as the name indicates, values that can be provided as inputs to runbooks and shared between them. Variables are particularly useful when a certain set of values should be shared among multiple jobs or runbooks.

A variable can also be defined inside a runbook, but the scope of the variable is then restricted inside that particular runbook. This is different from variables that are defined from the portal, which are persistent outside the scope of the runbook. The values can be set by runbooks and used by another runbook or DSC configuration. Since the values are persistent, they can also be used by runbooks the next time they are executed

Creating a Variable from the Portal

It is quite easy to create a variable from within the portal:

1. From the Automation account, scroll down to Shared Resources ➤ Variables. Then click the Add a Variable option (Figure 2-18).

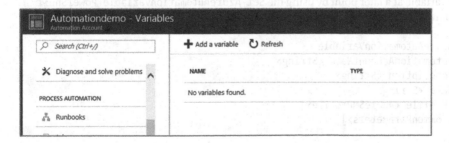

Figure 2-18. Adding a new variable

2.   Enter the Name, Description, Type, and Value (Figure 2-19).

Figure 2-19. *Variable details*

The type of variables can be String, Boolean, DateTime, Integer, or Not Specified. If Not Specified is used, the value of the variable will be set as NULL. You can set the value of the variable at a later point by using the Set-AzureAutomationVariable PowerShell command. The syntax for the command is as follows:

```
Set-AzureAutomationVariable
    -AutomationAccountName <String>
    -Description <String>
    -Name <String>
    [-Profile <AzureSMProfile>]
    [<CommonParameters>]
```

By default, the variables are not created as encrypted. However, you can choose to encrypt the variables, if required, during creation. If encrypted, the variable can be retrieved only from within a runbook by using the Get-AutomationVariable activity.

Managing Variables by Using PowerShell

You can create and manage Azure Automation variables by using PowerShell. You should be logged in to your Azure account via Azure PowerShell (Figure 2-20).

```
PS C:\WINDOWS\system32> Login-AzureRmAccount
```

Figure 2-20. *Logging into an Azure account via Azure PowerShell*

Provide the Azure login credentials when prompted.

The Get-AzureRmAutomationVariable command will get the values of a given Azure Automation account variable (Figure 2-21). The syntax is as follows:

```
Get-AzureRmAutomationVariable
    [-ResourceGroupName] <String>
    [-AutomationAccountName] <String>
    [-Name] <String>
    [<CommonParameters>]
```

```
PS C:\WINDOWS\system32> Get-AzureRmAutomationVariable

cmdlet Get-AzureRmAutomationVariable at command pipeline position 1
Supply values for the following parameters:
(Type !? for Help.)
ResourceGroupName: automationrg
AutomationAccountName: Automationdemo


Value                 : temp
Encrypted             : False  ■
ResourceGroupName     : automationrg
AutomationAccountName : Automationdemo
Name                  : Variable1
CreationTime          : 4/15/2017 6:23:17 AM +01:00
LastModifiedTime      : 4/15/2017 6:23:17 AM +01:00
Description           : Test variable
```

Figure 2-21. *Get-AzureRMAutomationVariable command output*

The command pulls out the available variables in the given Automation account.

You can pull out information on a specific variable independently and store it in another variable during runtime by using the commands shown in Figure 2-22.

```
PS C:\WINDOWS\system32> $Variable = Get-AzureRmAutomationVariable -AutomationAccountName "Automationdemo" -ResourceGrou
Name "Automationrg" -Name "Variable1"
PS C:\WINDOWS\system32> $value = $Variable.value
PS C:\WINDOWS\system32> $value
temp
```

Figure 2-22. *Variable runtime manipulation*

Similarly, you can also create new variables via PowerShell by using the New-AzureRmAutomationVariable command. The syntax is shown here:

```
New-AzureRmAutomationVariable
    [-ResourceGroupName] <String>
    [-AutomationAccountName] <String>
    [-Name] <String>
    [-Description <String>]
    -Encrypted <Boolean>
    [-Value <Object>]
    [<CommonParameters>]
```

In Figure 2-23, the command is executed against the target Automation account name and resource group with the name and value of the new variable.

```
PS C:\WINDOWS\system32> New-AzureRmAutomationVariable -AutomationAccountName "Automationdemo" -Name "Variable2" -Encrypt
ed $False -Value "test2" -ResourceGroupName "Automationrg"

Value                 : test2
Encrypted             : False
ResourceGroupName     : Automationrg
AutomationAccountName : Automationdemo
Name                  : Variable2
CreationTime          : 4/15/2017 6:36:16 AM +01:00
LastModifiedTime      : 4/15/2017 6:36:16 AM +01:00
Description           :
```

Figure 2-23. *Creating a new Automation variable*

You can go back to the portal and check, and the variable will be listed there (Figure 2-24).

NAME	TYPE	VALUE	LAST MODIFIED
Variable1	String	temp	4/15/2017 8:23 AM
Variable2	String	test2	4/15/2017 6:36 AM

➕ Add a variable ↻ Refresh

Figure 2-24. *List of variables in the Azure portal*

The Set-AzureRmAutomationVariable command can also be used to set the value of an existing variable (Figure 2-25).

```
PS C:\WINDOWS\system32> Set-AzureRmAutomationVariable -AutomationAccountName "Automationdemo" -Name "Variable1" -Resourc
eGroupName "Automationrg" -Value "Test1" -Encrypted $False

Value                 : Test1
Encrypted             : False
ResourceGroupName     : Automationrg
AutomationAccountName : Automationdemo
Name                  : Variable1
CreationTime          : 4/15/2017 6:23:17 AM +01:00
LastModifiedTime      : 4/15/2017 6:42:44 AM +01:00
Description           : Test variable
```

Figure 2-25. *Setting the value of an Azure Automation variable*

Here you can see that the value of the variable that we originally set from the Azure portal is set to Test1.

You can delete the variables by using the `Remove-AzureRmAutomationVariable` command. The syntax is as follows:

```
Remove-AzureRmAutomationVariable
        [-ResourceGroupName] <String>
        [-AutomationAccountName] <String>
        [-Name] <String>
        [-Force]
        [-Confirm]
        [-WhatIf]
        [<CommonParameters>]
```

You can provide mandatory parameters such as Automation account name, resource group name, and variable name to delete a variable (Figure 2-26).

```
PS C:\WINDOWS\system32> Remove-AzureRmAutomationVariable -AutomationAccountName "Automationdemo" -Name "Variable2" -Forc
e -ResourceGroupName "Automationrg"
```

Figure 2-26. *Deleting an Azure Automation variable*

Using Encrypted Variables

Creating encrypted variables is easy from the portal; you set Encrypted to Yes in the portal. You will not be able to view the value of the encrypted variable from the portal (Figure 2-27).

NAME	TYPE	VALUE
Variable1	String	Test1
Variable3	Unknown (encrypted)	******************

➕ Add a variable ↻ Refresh

Figure 2-27. *Encrypted Variable*

The value cannot be retrieved by using the `Get-AzureRmAutomationVariable` command either (Figure 2-28).

```
PS C:\WINDOWS\system32> $Variable = Get-AzureRmAutomationVariable -AutomationAccountName "Automationdemo" -Name "Variab
3" -ResourceGroupName "Automationrg"
PS C:\WINDOWS\system32> $Value = $Variable.value
PS C:\WINDOWS\system32> $Value
PS C:\WINDOWS\system32>
```

Figure 2-28. *Encrypted variable runtime manipulation*

You can get the value from inside a runbook by using the `Get-AutomationVariable` activity.

Let's create a sample runbook to demonstrate this:

1. Choose Automation Accounts ➤ Runbooks ➤ Add a Runbook.

2. Select the option to create a new runbook rather than importing from the gallery, as shown in Figure 2-29.

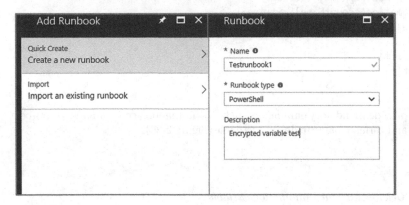

Figure 2-29. *Creating a new runbook*

3. This opens the Edit PowerShell Runbook pane. Type in **Get-AutomationVariable <Variablename>**.

4. Figure 2-30 shows the display of the value in the test pane.

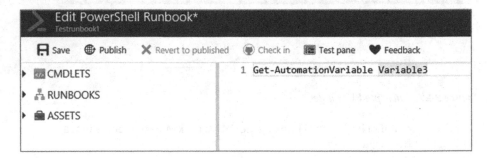

Figure 2-30. *Azure Automation runbook edit pane*

5. Click the Save option. Then click Test Pane and start the runbook.

There you can see that the activity pulls out the value of the encrypted variable (Figure 2-31).

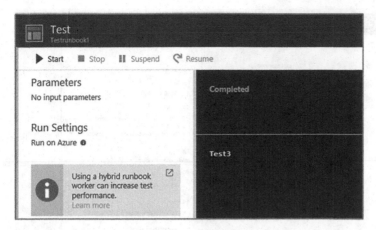

Figure 2-31. *Azure Automation runbook output*

Connections

The runbooks need to connect to various resources or external systems, and *connection* assets encapsulate the information required to enable this. The connection information could include username/password, subscription IDs, URLs, ports, and so forth. When you create the Azure Automation Run As accounts, two connection assets are created by default. You can view them from Automation account dashboard by choosing Assets ➤ Connections (Figure 2-32).

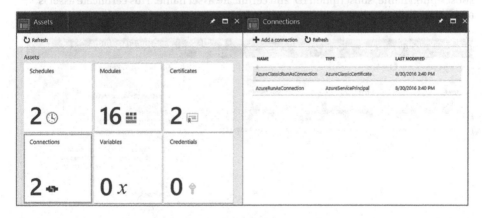

Figure 2-32. *Azure Automation connections list*

Let's look at these assets so you can understand how the connection assets work; see Figure 2-33.

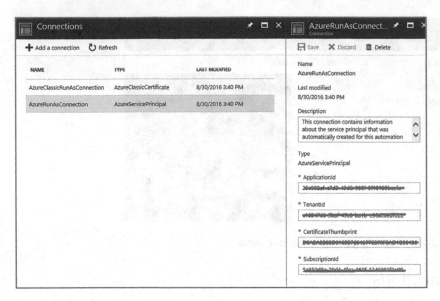

Figure 2-33. Connection information for AzureRunAsConnection

Here you can see the details of the service principal created in Azure AD for the Automation Run As account. This information includes the application ID, tenant ID, certificate thumbprint, and subscription ID.

When it comes to the classic connection asset, the parameters will be the subscription name, subscription ID, and certificate asset name. This certificate asset is also created automatically when you create the Run As account (Figure 2-34).

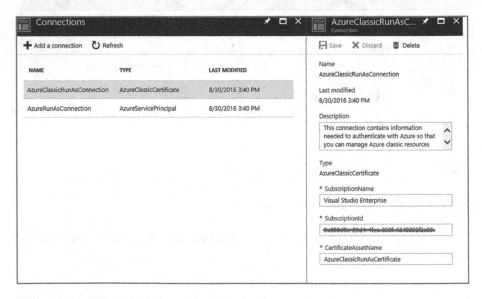

Figure 2-34. Connection information for AzureClassicRunAsConnection

Each connection is associated with a connection type, and each connection type is defined in integration modules. You can make your own PowerShell modules and include them in Azure Automation as integration modules. In addition to the PowerShell module, the integration module can optionally contain a metadata file that specifies the connection type to be used in Azure Automation. Integration modules provide the flexibility of bringing your own PowerShell modules to Azure when the required modules are not available by default. The modules that are available by default are called *global modules*. The modules imported by users takes precedence over the global modules.

Creating a New Connection

From the Automation account dashboard, choose Assets ➤ Connections ➤ Add a Connection. Depending on the type of connection selected, you need to provide additional inputs (Figure 2-35).

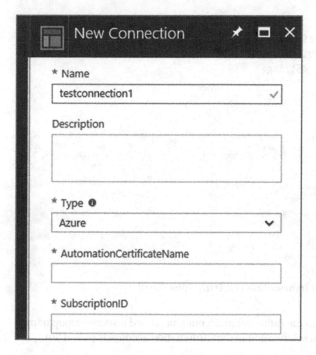

Figure 2-35. New connection details

In this example, I have selected the connection type as Azure, and this option prompts for entering the Automation certificate name and the subscription ID.

Managing Connections by Using PowerShell

You can use Azure PowerShell to manage connection assets.

Get-AzureRmAutomationConnection

The Get-AzureRmAutomationConnection command gets information about connections in each automation account (Figure 2-36).

The syntax of this command is as follows:

```
Get-AzureRmAutomationConnection
    [-ResourceGroupName] <String>
    [-AutomationAccountName] <String>
    [-ConnectionTypeName] <String>
    [<CommonParameters>]

Or:
Get-AzureRmAutomationConnection
    [-ResourceGroupName] <String>
    [-AutomationAccountName] <String>
    [-Name] <String>
    [<CommonParameters>]
```

```
PS C:\WINDOWS\system32>
PS C:\WINDOWS\system32> Get-AzureRmAutomationConnection -ResourceGroupName "Automationrg" -AutomationAccountName "Automa
tiondemo"

ConnectionTypeName    : AzureClassicCertificate
FieldDefinitionValues : {}
ResourceGroupName     : Automationrg
AutomationAccountName : Automationdemo
Name                  : AzureClassicRunAsConnection
CreationTime          : 4/9/2017 8:40:19 AM +01:00
LastModifiedTime      : 4/9/2017 8:40:19 AM +01:00
Description           :

ConnectionTypeName    : AzureServicePrincipal
FieldDefinitionValues : {}
ResourceGroupName     : Automationrg
AutomationAccountName : Automationdemo
Name                  : AzureRunAsConnection
CreationTime          : 4/9/2017 8:40:42 AM +01:00
LastModifiedTime      : 4/9/2017 8:40:42 AM +01:00
Description           :
```

Figure 2-36. *Getting connection information via Azure PowerShell*

If you run the command with the Automation account name and resource group name as parameters, all the connection information in that Automation account is pulled out.

New-AzureRmAutomationConnection

The New-AzureRmAutomationConnection command is for creating a new connection.

The syntax is as follows:

```
New-AzureRmAutomationConnection
    [-ResourceGroupName] <String>
    [-AutomationAccountName] <String>
```

```
[-Name] <String>
[-ConnectionTypeName] <String>
[-ConnectionFieldValues] <IDictionary>
[-Description <String>]
[<CommonParameters>]
```

Let's create a new connection asset by using PowerShell. In the first command, the connection field values (the certificate name and the subscription ID) are provided. This information is called in the New-AzureRmAutomationConnection command to create the connection asset (Figure 2-37).

```
PS C:\WINDOWS\system32>
>> $FieldValues = @{"AutomationCertificateName"="AzureClassicRunAsCertificate";"SubscriptionID"="5a850d8e-29d4-4fea-850f
-1340392f2a99"}
PS C:\WINDOWS\system32> New-AzureRmAutomationConnection -Name "Connection1" -ConnectionTypeName Azure -ConnectionFieldVa
lues $FieldValues -ResourceGroupName "Automationrg" -AutomationAccountName "Automationdemo"

ConnectionTypeName   : Azure
FieldDefinitionValues : {AutomationCertificateName, SubscriptionID}
ResourceGroupName    : Automationrg
AutomationAccountName : Automationdemo
Name                 : Connection1
CreationTime         : 4/15/2017 6:24:20 PM +01:00
LastModifiedTime     : 4/15/2017 6:24:20 PM +01:00
Description          :
```

Figure 2-37. *Creating a new connection via Azure PowerShell*

You can see that the asset is listed in the portal after it's created (Figure 2-38).

NAME	TYPE
AzureClassicRunAsConnection	AzureClassicCertificate
AzureRunAsConnection	AzureServicePrincipal
Connection1	Azure

➕ Add a connection   ⟳ Refresh

Figure 2-38. *Connection list in the Azure portal*

Remove-AzureRmAutomationConnection

As the name indicates, the Remove-AzureRmAutomationConnection command deletes an existing connection from the Automation account.

The syntax is as follows:

```
Remove-AzureRmAutomationConnection
    [-ResourceGroupName] <String>
    [-AutomationAccountName] <String>
    [-Name] <String>
    [-Force]
```

```
[-Confirm]
[-WhatIf]
[<CommonParameters>]
```

The command deletes the newly created connection asset, as shown in Figure 2-39.

```
PS C:\WINDOWS\system32> Remove-AzureRmAutomationConnection -AutomationAccountName "Automationdemo" -Name "Connection1"
ResourceGroupName "Automationrg"

Confirm
Are you sure you want to remove the Azure Automation Connection ?
[Y] Yes  [N] No  [S] Suspend  [?] Help (default is "Y"): Y
PS C:\WINDOWS\system32>
```

Figure 2-39. *Removing a connection via Azure PowerShell*

Set-AzureRmAutomationConnectionFieldValue

Another command, Set-AzureRmAutomationConnectionFieldValue, can set the values of a field for a connection asset.

Here is the syntax:

```
Set-AzureRmAutomationConnectionFieldValue
    [-ResourceGroupName] <String>
    [-AutomationAccountName] <String>
    [-Name] <String>
    -ConnectionFieldName <String>
    -Value <Object>
    [<CommonParameters>]
```

In the example in Figure 2-40, the command is used to update the certificate name of the connection asset named Connection2.

```
PS C:\WINDOWS\system32> Set-AzureRmAutomationConnectionFieldValue -Name "Connection2" -ConnectionFieldName "AutomationCe
rtificateName" -Value "AzureClassicRunAsCertificate" -ResourceGroupName "Automationrg" -AutomationAccountName "Automatic
ndemo"

ConnectionTypeName    : Azure
FieldDefinitionValues : {AutomationCertificateName, SubscriptionID}
ResourceGroupName     : Automationrg
AutomationAccountName : Automationdemo
Name                  : Connection2
CreationTime          : 4/15/2017 6:31:42 PM +01:00
LastModifiedTime      : 4/15/2017 6:33:12 PM +01:00
Description           :
```

Figure 2-40. *Setting a connection value via PowerShell*

Get-AutomationConnection

The activity named Get-AutomationConnection can be used to get information about the connection from within a runbook.

Let's create a runbook with the type PowerShell to test this out. Call the activity with the connection name and parameter to retrieve information about the connection (Figure 2-41).

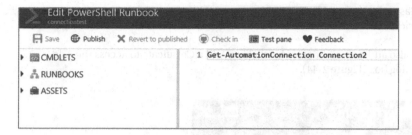

Figure 2-41. *Azure Automation runbook edit pane*

You can save the runbook and execute it in the Test pane to view the results (Figure 2-42).

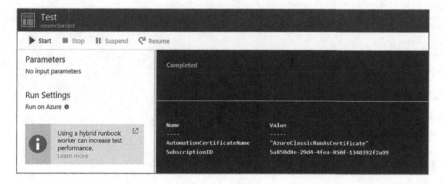

Figure 2-42. *Runbook test result*

Certificates

Certificate assets authenticate the access of runbooks to various resources in Azure, including ARM and classic resources. When the Azure Automation Run As account is created, two certificate assets are created by default. You can view these assets from the Automation account dashboard by choosing Assets ➤ Certificates (Figure 2-43).

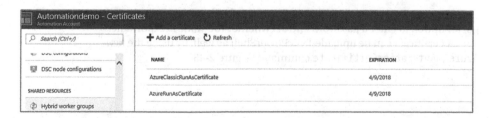

Figure 2-43. *Azure Automation certificates list*

AzureClassicRunAsCertificate, as the name indicates, authenticates access to manage classic resources. AzureRunAsCertificate authenticates access to manage ARM resources.

You can also add new certificates by clicking Add a Certificate to access the Add a Certificate dialog box (Figure 2-44).

Figure 2-44. *New certificate details*

You can choose to upload a .cer file or a .pfx file. If you upload a .pfx file, you will get an option to enter a password and set whether the value is exportable.

A certificate can be uploaded via PowerShell as well, by using the New-AzureRmAutomationCertificate command (Figure 2-45).

The syntax is as follows:

```
New-AzureRmAutomationCertificate
    [-ResourceGroupName] <String>
    [-AutomationAccountName] <String>
    [-Name] <String>
    [-Path] <String>
    [-Description <String>]
    [-Exportable]
    [-Password <SecureString>]
    [<CommonParameters>]
```

```
PS C:\> $certname = "TestCertificate"
PS C:\> $certpath ='.\ClientCertificateName.pfx"
PS C:\> $certpwd = ConvertTo-SecureString -String 'P@ssw0rd1' -AsPlainText -Force
PS C:\> $ResourceGroup = 'Automationrg'
PS C:\> New-AzureRmAutomationCertificate -AutomationAccountName "Automationdemo" -Name $certName -Path $certPath -Passwo
rd $certPwd -Exportable -ResourceGroupName $ResourceGroup
>>

Thumbprint             : 32602A3CA8D2C818394EA436D67EC13ECEEF3CFD
Exportable             : True
ExpiryTime             : 11/15/2024 3:43:14 AM +00:00
ResourceGroupName      : Automationrg
AutomationAccountName  : Automationdemo
Name                   : TestCertificate
CreationTime           : 4/15/2017 7:31:50 PM +01:00
LastModifiedTime       : 4/15/2017 7:31:50 PM +01:00
Description            :
```

Figure 2-45. *Creating a new certificate via Azure PowerShell*

Execute the command with certificate information and Automation account information as parameters.

You can use the certificate from within a runbook by using the Get-AutomationCertificate activity. Create a new runbook and call the activity with certificate name as a parameter (Figure 2-46).

```
Edit PowerShell Runbook
Certtest

  Save    Publish    Revert to published    Check in    Test pane    Feedback

▶  CMDLETS                    1  Get-AutomationCertificate ClientCertificateName
▶  RUNBOOKS
▶  ASSETS
```

Figure 2-46. *Azure Automation runbook edit pane*

You can run a test execution to review the output values (Figure 2-47).

Figure 2-47. *Test execution output*

Credentials

The credential asset in Azure Automation is same as the PowerShell `PSCredential` object holding security credentials for authenticating against a service. These credentials can be called by runbooks for authentication purposes.

Creating credential objects from the portal is straightforward. Go to the Azure Automation dashboard and choose Assets ➤ Credentials ➤ Add a Credential to access the New Credential dialog box (Figure 2-48).

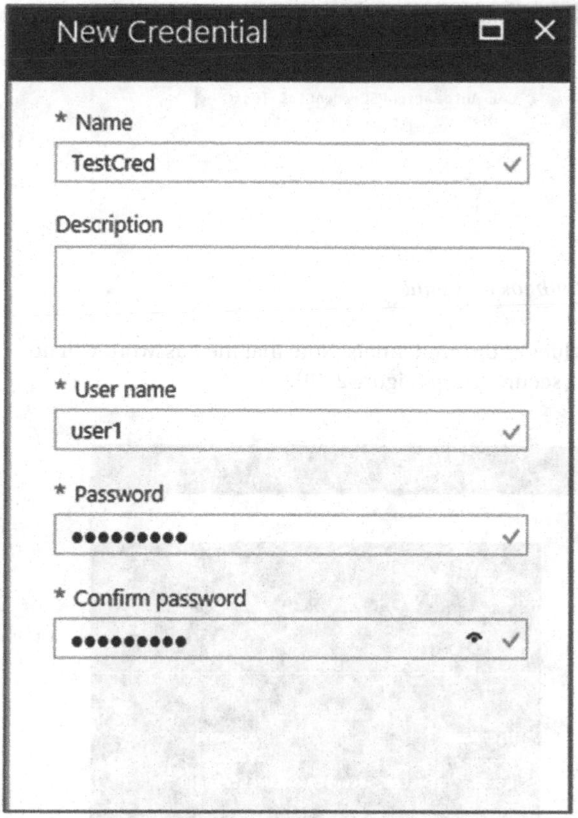

Figure 2-48. *New credential details*

You can also provide a username in the format *domain\username* or *username@domain*.

The value of a credential can be viewed by using the `Get-AutomationPSCredential` workflow from within a runbook.

Similar to the examples mentioned earlier for other assets, you can create a runbook with the `Get-AutomationPSCredential` activity and the credential name (Figure 2-49).

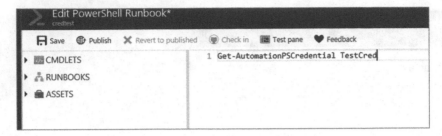

Figure 2-49. *Azure Automation Runbook edit pane*

Execute the runbook to get values of the credentials. Note that the password will not be displayed because it is stored as secure string (Figure 2-50).

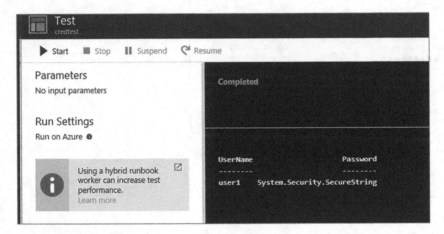

Figure 2-50. *Azure Automation runbook output*

Nested Runbooks

Along with the various Automation assets, nested runbooks are another Azure Automation feature that enables modularity. You can define commonly executed tasks as a runbook and then call it as a child runbook from various parent runbooks. There are two ways to call a child runbook: either by invoking the child runbook inline or by using the Start-AzureRMAutomationRunbook PowerShell cmdlet.

Invoking a Child Runbook Inline

Runbook inline invocation is the synchronous execution of a child runbook from a parent runbook. The parent runbook will wait for the execution of child runbook to be completed before moving on to the next line of code. Only a single Azure Automation job is created that takes care of the tasks defined in both child runbook and parent runbook.

The child runbook that is invoked inline should be published before the parent runbook. You can store the output of a child runbook in a variable while invoking it inline. The parameters for a child runbook can also be passed on by using variables. However, the name of a child runbook cannot be passed on using a variable and should be explicitly named inside the parent runbook. The execution of child and parent runbook is covered in a single job, which makes debugging easier.

From the edit pane of the parent runbook, you can directly add a child runbook from the same Automation account via the Add to Canvas option (Figure 2-51).

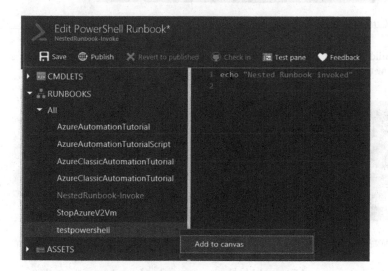

Figure 2-51. *Adding a child runbook to the canvas*

This option will add the child runbook to the parent runbook from which it is invoked (Figure 2-52).

Figure 2-52. *Inserting the child runbook*

To keep the example simple, I have included an echo command in the child runbook so that the execution order is clear (Figure 2-53).

Figure 2-53. *Contents of the child runbook*

Publish the child runbook first, followed by the parent runbook. Now start the parent runbook and review the output (Figure 2-54).

Figure 2-54. *Invoke method output*

The child runbook is executed from within the parent runbook, and we can see the results in the same output window.

If you check the jobs associated with the child runbook, no jobs will be listed (Figure 2-55), because the execution happens from within the parent runbook job.

Figure 2-55. *The child runbook's job list*

Starting a Runbook by Using Start-AzureRMAutomationRunbook

Start-AzureRMAutomation command can be used to initiate an asynchronous execution of a child runbook when it is called from within the parent runbook. Any runbook execution initiated by using Start-AzureRMAutomationRunbook will run as a separate job, independent of the parent runbook from which it is called. The name of the runbook can be passed on as a parameter, and the job status can also be stored in a variable. While the parent runbook will continue to execute the next line of code after starting the child runbook, the job status can be leveraged to delay this execution. The Get-AzureRMAutomationJobOutput command can be used to extract the output of a child runbook that is started with the Start-AzureRMAutomationRunbook command. The debugging of the child runbook and parent runbook will be slightly difficult compared to the invoking method, because multiple jobs are created during the execution. Unlike the previous option, the child runbook in this method is not limited to the same Automation account. You can call runbooks from different Automation accounts or even different subscriptions, provided the connection asset to that subscription is available.

The contents of a sample parent runbook that calls a child runbook by using Start-AzureRMAutomationRunbook is shown here:

```
$connectionName = "AzureRunAsConnection"
try
{
    # Get the connection "AzureRunAsConnection "
    $servicePrincipalConnection=Get-AutomationConnection -Name
    $connectionName

    "Logging in to Azure..."
    Add-AzureRmAccount `
        -ServicePrincipal `
        -TenantId $servicePrincipalConnection.TenantId `
        -ApplicationId $servicePrincipalConnection.ApplicationId `
        -CertificateThumbprint $servicePrincipalConnection.
        CertificateThumbprint
}
catch {
    if (!$servicePrincipalConnection)
    {
        $ErrorMessage = "Connection $connectionName not found."
        throw $ErrorMessage
    } else{
        Write-Error -Message $_.Exception
        throw $_.Exception
    }
}
```

```
#Start runbook by using the Start-AzureRmAutomationRunbook command with the
#resource group name, runbook name, and automation account name as input
parameters
Start-AzureRmAutomationRunbook -ResourceGroupName 'sccmrg' -Name
'testpowershell' -AutomationAccountName 'hybriddemo'
```

As you can see in this code, it is necessary to connect to the Azure subscription first by using the AzureRunASConnection credentials before you can use the Start-AzureRmAutomationRunbook command.

The output of the runbook is shown in Figure 2-56.

Figure 2-56. *Runbook output*

Note that the output of the child runbook is not listed. While using the invoke method, both parent and child runbook were executed from the same job, and you could see the output in one place.

However, if you check the job list associated with the child runbook, you can see that it has been executed separately (Figure 2-57).

Figure 2-57. *Child runbook job list*

You need to check the job details of the child runbook to view its output (Figure 2-58).

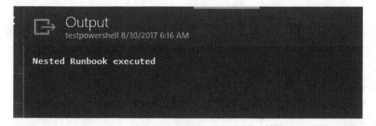

Figure 2-58. *Child runbook output*

Summary

This chapter explained the various Azure automation assets, their properties, and how to leverage them while creating runbooks. This chapter also explained how to implement modularity by leveraging nested runbooks. The next chapter explores the various Azure runbook types in detail.

■ Additional References

https://azure.microsoft.com/en-in/blog/getting-started-with-azure-automation-automation-assets-2/

https://docs.microsoft.com/en-in/azure/automation/automation-credentials

https://docs.microsoft.com/en-in/azure/automation/automation-certificates

https://docs.microsoft.com/en-in/azure/automation/automation-schedules

CHAPTER 3

■ ■ ■

Azure Automation Runbook Types

Azure Automation uses Four types of runbooks, as briefly introduced in Chapter 1: PowerShell, PowerShell Workflow, Graphical and Graphical PowerShell Workflow. This chapter offers a deep dive into each of these runbook types and shows how to get started with them. You'll also learn how to create, import, edit, test, and publish runbooks in an Automation account. Note that the Graphical and Graphical PowerShell Workflow runbooks have almost similar properties with exception that the latter uses PowerShell Workflow in the backend. Hence we will be focussing only on Graphical runbooks among the two in this chapter.

PowerShell Runbooks

PowerShell runbooks are PowerShell scripts that can be executed against Azure resources. You can either import your own PowerShell script or use one from the PowerShell Gallery or Script Center. After importing the runbooks, you can edit them directly from the Runbook Gallery.

Let's import a PowerShell script directly from the Azure gallery. Go to Automation dashboard and choose Runbooks ➤ Browse Gallery. For the Gallery Source, select Script Center, Type as PowerShell script and Publisher as Microsoft (Figure 3-1).

© Shijimol Ambi Karthikeyan 2017
S. Ambi Karthikeyan, *Azure Automation Using the ARM Model*,
https://doi.org/10.1007/978-1-4842-3219-4_3

Figure 3-1. *Selecting the PowerShell Script option*

I chose Microsoft as the Publisher for this demonstration.

Select the runbook to be imported. In this case, I am going to import a simple PowerShell runbook from the gallery that starts Azure VMs in a subscription or cloud service (Figure 3-2).

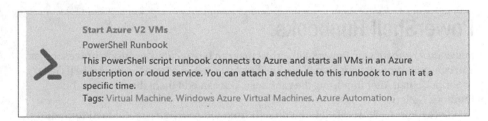

Figure 3-2. *Selecting a sample runbook*

Once the runbook is imported, by default the edit pane will open. On the left side of the edit panel, you can view all the available components for the runbook, listed as CMDLETS, RUNBOOKS, and ASSETS (Figure 3-3).

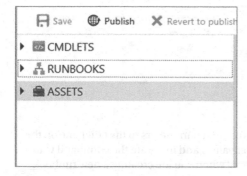

Figure 3-3. *Runbook components*

If you expand CMDLETS, you can view details of all the modules imported for that runbook (Figure 3-4).

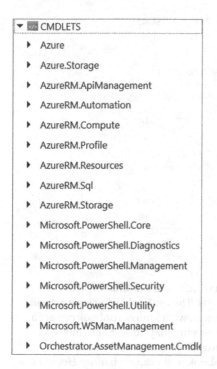

Figure 3-4. *Available modules*

If you want to customize the runbook and add a command from one of those modules, you can click the command and select the Add to Canvas option (Figure 3-5).

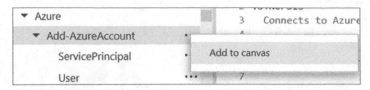

Figure 3-5. Adding the command to the canvas

This copies over the command with the required parameters to the edit pane on the right-hand side. You can update the parameter values and integrate the command with the script logic. This feature is particularly useful when you are creating a new runbook on your own.

The RUNBOOKS component in the left panel lists the runbooks that are currently available in the Automation account (Figure 3-6).

RUNBOOKS		
▼ All	3	Calcu
	4	.DESCRIPT
Add-DataDiskToRmVM •••	5	Enume
AzureAutomationTutorial •	Add to canvas	
AzureAutomationTutorialScript •••	9	
AzureClassicAutomationTutorial •••	10	The d
	11	http:
AzureClassicAutomationTutorial •••	12	
CalculateBlobCost	13	Note:
	14	can b
scaleUpV2Vm •••	15	Set-A
StopAzureV2Vm •••	16	.EXAMPLE

Figure 3-6. Adding the runbook to the canvas

If you want to call any of these runbooks from within your Automation account, you can click that runbook and choose Add to Canvas. The runbook being inserted will act as a child runbook. There are certain restrictions on what kind of runbook can act as a child runbook. PowerShell-based runbooks such as pure play PowerShell runbooks and Graphical runbooks can call each other. The Workflow runbooks (PowerShell Workflow and Graphical PowerShell Workflow runbooks) can call each other. However, to call a PowerShell runbook from within a PowerShell Workflow runbook, the Start-AzureRMAutomationRunbook command should be used, and vice versa.

Let's insert a PowerShell child runbook from within another PowerShell runbook (Figure 3-7).

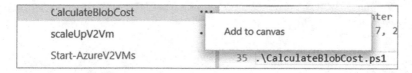

Figure 3-7. Adding a child runbook to the canvas

You can see that it is inserted as .\CalaculateBlobCost.ps1.

In the Assets section, you can view all assets related to that specific Automation account (Figure 3-8).

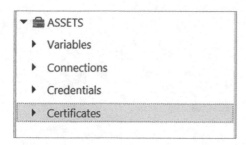

Figure 3-8. Runbook Assets list

You can add the assets to the runbook again by selecting the Add to Canvas option. When you insert the assets, they will be inserted using the corresponding activity (Figure 3-9).

```
35   Get-AutomationCertificate -Name 'AzureClassicRunAsCertificate'
36
37   Get-AutomationPSCredential -Name 'testcred'
38
39   Get-AutomationConnection -Name 'AzureClassicRunAsConnection'
40
```

Figure 3-9. Assets inserted to canvas

As you can see, editing the runbooks from the portal is thus made easy with many point-and-play features that help you customize the runbooks.

The best practice while creating runbooks is to give a description at the beginning of the runbook. Let's take a look at the runbook that we imported. It starts with the description that explains the runbook requirements in terms of inputs and expected outputs (Figure 3-10).

```
1  <#
2  .SYNOPSIS
3    Connects to Azure and starts of all VMs in the specified Azure subscription or resource group
4
5  .DESCRIPTION
6    This runbook connects to Azure and starts all VMs in an Azure subscription or resource group.
7    You can attach a schedule to this runbook to run it at a specific time. Note that this runbook does not start
8    Azure classic VMs. Use https://gallery.technet.microsoft.com/scriptcenter/Start-Azure-Classic-VMs-86ef746b for that.
9
10  REQUIRED AUTOMATION ASSETS
11    1. An Automation variable asset called "AzureSubscriptionId" that contains the GUID for this Azure subscription.
12       To use an asset with a different name you can pass the asset name as a runbook input parameter or change the default value for the input parameter.
13    2. An Automation credential asset called "AzureCredential" that contains the Azure AD user credential with authorization for this subscription.
14       To use an asset with a different name you can pass the asset name as a runbook input parameter or change the default value for the input parameter.
15
```

Figure 3-10. *Runbook description*

Before starting the runbook, the parameters can be defined. This is a recommended best practice if you want to reuse the runbook with different values each time that you run it (Figure 3-11).

```
36  param (
37      [Parameter(Mandatory=$false)]
38      [String]  $AzureCredentialAssetName = 'AzureCredential',
39
40      [Parameter(Mandatory=$false)]
41      [String] $AzureSubscriptionIdAssetName = 'AzureSubscriptionId',
42
43      [Parameter(Mandatory=$false)]
44      [String] $ResourceGroupName
45  )
```

Figure 3-11. *Runbook parameters*

Parameters are defined inside a param statement. You can indicate whether the parameters are mandatory. In this case, the parameter is not mandatory, and it will use the default values provided (AzureCredential and AzureSubscriptionId). If no default values are provided, as in the case of the parameter $ResourceGroupName, then a null value will be used. All these parameters are of the type String; hence the inputs provided during execution should be of the type String. The type will differ based on the input values that you want to provide. For example, if you are providing numeric values, you might want to add a parameter of type int.

Similarly, the OutputType command specifies the type of data returned by the script (Figure 3-12).

```
# Returns strings with status messages
[OutputType([String])]
```

Figure 3-12. *Runbook output type*

The Get-AutomationPSCredential activity is used here to get values of the Azure credential asset and pass it on to the Add-AzureRMAccount command for the authentication against the Azure subscription (Figure 3-13).

```
$Cred = Get-AutomationPSCredential -Name $AzureCredentialAssetName -ErrorAction Stop

$null = Add-AzureRmAccount -Credential $Cred -ErrorAction Stop -ErrorVariable err
if($err) {
    throw $err
}

$SubId = Get-AutomationVariable -Name $AzureSubscriptionIdAssetName -ErrorAction Stop
```

Figure 3-13. *Get Automation Credential asset values*

The subscription ID is again obtained from a variable asset.

Now the script moves on to the logical flow, wherein the target VMs are retrieved by using the Get-AzureRmVM command and then started by using the Start-AzureRmVM command (Figure 3-14).

```
# If there is a specific resource group, then get all VMs in the resource group,
# otherwise get all VMs in the subscription.
if ($ResourceGroupName)
{
    $VMs = Get-AzureRmVM -ResourceGroupName $ResourceGroupName
}
else
{
    $VMs = Get-AzureRmVM
}

# Start each of the VMs
foreach ($VM in $VMs)
{
    $StartRtn = $VM | Start-AzureRmVM -ErrorAction Continue

    if ($StartRtn.Status -ne 'Succeeded')
    {
        # The VM failed to start, so send notice
        Write-Output ($VM.Name + " failed to start")
        Write-Error ($VM.Name + " failed to start. Error was:") -ErrorAction Continue
        Write-Error (ConvertTo-Json $StartRtn.Error) -ErrorAction Continue
    }
    else
    {
        # The VM stopped, so send notice
        Write-Output ($VM.Name + " has been started")
    }
}
```

Figure 3-14. *Runbook logical workflow*

As you can see in the example, PowerShell scripts that you might be running from on-premises can be used as a runbook in Azure with minimal modification.

PowerShell Workflow Runbooks

To create a new *PowerShell Workflow*-based runbook, go to your Azure Automation account and choose Runbooks ➤ Add a Runbook. You can select the Quick Create option and set the runbook type as PowerShell Workflow.

PowerShell workflows are based on Windows Workflow Foundation. PowerShell Workflow based runbooks are slightly complex when compared to PowerShell runbooks and needs additional changes to convert the PowerShell script to a workflow. It is recommended to use workflows when you need checkpoints within the script or failure recovery, for example.

One visible difference between PowerShell runbooks and PowerShell Workflow-based runbooks is the usage of the Workflow keyword. The syntax is as follows:

```
Workflow <workflowname>
{
    <Commands>
}
```

The workflowname should be same as the runbook name. A workflow consists of activities executed one after the other. The PowerShell cmdlets are automatically converted to activities during execution.

InlineScript Activity

Some cmdlets that cannot be converted to an activity are run as is, using InlineScript. However, some cmdlets are excluded from this process and cannot be executed from within the script. You will get error messages if you try running those cmdlets from within the runbook directly. Hence an InlineScript block should be declared, and the commands should be executed from within the script block. The variables/parameters declared in the runbook elsewhere are not available inside the InlineScript block by default. If you want to call them within the InlineScript block, use the $Using scope modifier. A sample InlineScript block is shown here:

```
InlineScript{

        $Vnet =$Using:Vnet
        $ResourceGroup = $Using: ResourceGroup

$vnet = Get-AzureRmVirtualNetwork -Name $VNet -ResourceGroupName
$ResourceGroup

}
```

This script is calling the parameters $Vnet and $ResourceGroup declared outside the InlineScript block with the $Using scope definition.

Though InlineScript blocks are useful in many scenarios, some features of the workflow such as parallel execution and checkpoints are not available inside them.

Parallel Processing in the Workflow

One of the key features of workflows is the ability to execute activities in parallel. These activities should be defined inside a `parallel` script block inside the workflow:

```
Workflow test
parallel {

    Get-Process –Name PowerShell*

    Get-Service –Name s*

}
Write-output "Tasks completed"

}
```

Here the `Get-Process` and `Get-Service` commands are executed in parallel. Then the parallel block is exited, and the command to write the output is executed.

If you want to execute a set of commands against few targets concurrently, use the `foreach -parallel` construct. The syntax is as follows:

```
foreach -parallel ($<item> in $<collection>{

    sequence {

      <Activity1>
      <Activity2>

    }

}
```

Here `Activity1` and `Activity2` are executed against each item in the collection in parallel. However, their execution order against any particular item will be sequential.

Checkpoints in the Workflow

While running the activities in a workflow, exceptions could be thrown. Instead of executing the entire workflow from the beginning, you might want to resume the workflow from the point where the exception was thrown. Checkpoints are placed in the workflow to enable this. The command used is `checkpoint-workflow`. The syntax is as follows:

```
<Activity1>
checkpoint-workflow
<Activity2>
```

If an exception happens after `Activity1`, the workflow will start off from `Activity2` when you execute the workflow the next time.

Sample Use Case

The use case that I am going to discuss here is automated provisioning of VMs with the number of data disks that you define. You can also specify the size of the data disks to be provisioned. In Azure, you can attach data disks from the portal only after the VM creation. Here we are automating the same process, wherein the VMs can be provisioned with data disks already attached.

There is no runbook readily available in the gallery to do this task. Therefore, an Azure PowerShell script to create a new Azure VM in the ARM portal was tweaked to achieve this: https://msdn.microsoft.com/en-us/library/mt603754.aspx.

The tweaks include the following:

> Converted the PowerShell script to workflow.

> Minor changes to use existing storage and network.

> Commands to add data disk.

> Had to introduce InlineScript in the workflow so that the PowerShell commands are executed independently. If this is not done, it will throw errors due to issues in data conversion.

> Introduced basic for loop to add data disks based on provisioning requirements.

Here is the runbook:

Runbook:

```
===============================================================
workflow dynamicDDwithparamter
  {

        param (

        # If you do not enter anything, the default values will be taken

        # VM name, availability set, and NIC card name

        [parameter(Mandatory=$true)]

        [String]$VMName,

        [parameter(Mandatory=$true)]

        [String]$ComputerName,

        [parameter(Mandatory=$true)]

        [String]$AvailabilitySetname,
```

```
[parameter(Mandatory=$true)]

[String]$InterfaceName,

## Compute - Name of VM to be created,Vm size, data disk name

[parameter(Mandatory=$true)]

[String]$UserName,

[parameter(Mandatory=$true)]

[String]$Password,

## Storage - Name of existing storage

[parameter(Mandatory=$true)]

[String]$StorageName = "testsql295p",

## Global - Uses an existing resource group

[parameter(Mandatory=$true)]

[String]$ResourceGroupName = "autotest",

[parameter(Mandatory=$true)]

[String]$Location = "WestEurope",

## Network - Name of existing network. This should match the network
#settings of other VMs in the target availability set

[parameter(Mandatory=$true)]

[String]$Subnet1Name = "Subnet1",

[parameter(Mandatory=$true)]

[String]$VNetName = "VNet10",

[parameter(Mandatory=$true)]

## Datadisk - Provide number of data disks and size of the disks

[Int]$Disknumber ,

[parameter(Mandatory=$true)]
```

```
        [Int]$DisksizeinGB ,

        ## Compute - VM size

        [parameter(Mandatory=$true)]

        [String]$VMSize = "Standard_A2"

    )

    InlineScript{

        $VMName =$Using:VMName

        $StorageName = $Using:StorageName

        $ResourceGroupName = $Using:ResourceGroupName

        $Location = $Using:Location

        $InterfaceName = $Using:InterfaceName

        $Subnet1Name = $Using:Subnet1Name

        $VNetName = $Using:VNetName

        $ComputerName = $Using:ComputerName

        $VMSize = $Using:VMSize

        $AvailabilitySetname = $Using:AvailabilitySetname

        $UserName = $Using:UserName

        $Password = $Using:Password

        $Disknumber = $Using:Disknumber

        $DisksizeinGB =$Using:DisksizeinGB

$connectionName = "AzureRunAsConnection"
    # Get the connection "AzureRunAsConnection "
    $servicePrincipalConnection=Get-AutomationConnection -Name
    $connectionName
    "Logging in to Azure..."
    Add-AzureRmAccount `

        -ServicePrincipal `
```

```
            -TenantId $servicePrincipalConnection.TenantId `

            -ApplicationId $servicePrincipalConnection.ApplicationId `

            -CertificateThumbprint $servicePrincipalConnection.
            CertificateThumbprint


$OSDiskName = $VMName + "OSDisk"


$dataDiskName = $VMName + "DataDisk"


$StorageAccount = Get-AzureRmStorageAccount -ResourceGroupName
$ResourceGroupName -AccountName $StorageName


"Collected storage account details ..."
# Network - Creates Public IP, NIC card, and get VNet details
 "configure NIC..."


$PIp = New-AzureRmPublicIpAddress -Name $InterfaceName -ResourceGroupName
$ResourceGroupName -Location $Location -AllocationMethod Dynamic -Force


$vnet = Get-AzureRmVirtualNetwork -Name $VNetName -ResourceGroupName
$ResourceGroupName


$subnetconfig = Get-AzureRmVirtualNetworkSubnetConfig -VirtualNetwork $vnet


$Interface = New-AzureRmNetworkInterface -Name $InterfaceName
-ResourceGroupName $ResourceGroupName -Location $Location -SubnetId $VNet.
Subnets[0].Id -PublicIpAddressId $PIp.Id -Force


# Compute configuration
## Set up local VM object
 "creating VM object properties..."


$secpasswd = ConvertTo-SecureString $Password -AsPlainText -Force


$mycreds = New-Object System.Management.Automation.PSCredential ($UserName,
$secpasswd)


$AvailabilitySet = Get-AzureRmAvailabilitySet -ResourceGroupName
$resourcegroupName -Name $AvailabilitySetname


$VirtualMachine = New-AzureRmVMConfig -VMName $VMName -VMSize $VMSize
-availabilitysetID $AvailabilitySet.id


$VirtualMachine = Set-AzureRmVMOperatingSystem -VM $VirtualMachine -Windows
-ComputerName $ComputerName -Credential $mycreds -ProvisionVMAgent
-EnableAutoUpdate
```

71

```
$VirtualMachine = Set-AzureRmVMSourceImage -VM $VirtualMachine
-PublisherName MicrosoftWindowsServer -Offer WindowsServer -Skus 2012-R2-
Datacenter -Version "latest"

$VirtualMachine = Add-AzureRmVMNetworkInterface -VM $VirtualMachine -Id
$Interface.Id

$OSDiskUri = $StorageAccount.PrimaryEndpoints.Blob.ToString() + "vhds/" +
$OSDiskName + ".vhd"

$VirtualMachine = Set-AzureRmVMOSDisk -VM $VirtualMachine -Name $OSDiskName
-VhdUri $OSDiskUri -CreateOption FromImage
 # Attach Data Disks

For ($i=1; $i -le $Disknumber; $i++) {
    $dataDiskName = $dataDiskName + $i

   $DataDiskVhdUri01 = $StorageAccount.PrimaryEndpoints.Blob.ToString() +
   "vhds/" + $dataDiskName + ".vhd"

   $VirtualMachine = Add-AzureRmVMDataDisk -VM $VirtualMachine -Name
   $dataDiskName -Caching 'ReadOnly' -DiskSizeInGB $DisksizeinGB -Lun $i
   -VhdUri $DataDiskVhdUri01 -CreateOption Empty

   $dataDiskName = $VMName + "DataDisk"

    }

"created VM object properties..."
## Create the VM in Azure
 "creating Virtual machine..."

New-AzureRmVM -ResourceGroupName $ResourceGroupName -Location $Location -VM
$VirtualMachine

"created Virtual machine..."

    }

}
================================================================================
```

Graphical Runbooks

Graphical runbooks use a point-and-play model, which makes it easier for administrators to create and execute them with minimal PowerShell knowledge. Even though Graphical runbooks use PowerShell under the hood, the process is transparent to the user.

You can either import a runbook from the gallery or create a new one from your Automation account by choosing Runbooks ➤ Add a Runbook. Set the runbook type to Graphical Workflow. The library items on the left panel are same as discussed earlier for the PowerShell runbook, except that it has an additional RUNBOOK CONTROL item available (Figure 3-15).

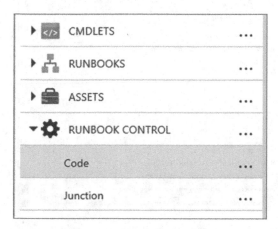

Figure 3-15. *Runbook control asset*

Runbook control activity includes Code and Junction activity types. The Code activity can be used when you want to insert a set of PowerShell commands in the workflow. If you add the code to the canvas and edit the same, you will get an option to insert the PowerShell cmdlets (Figure 3-16).

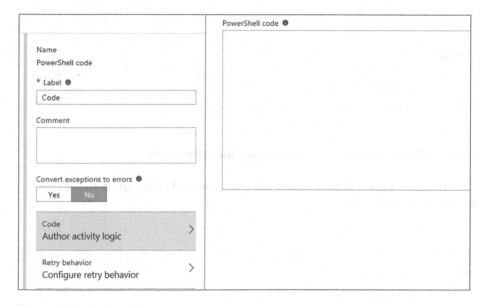

Figure 3-16. *Code activity*

73

You can also configure a retry logic for the code block (Figure 3-17).

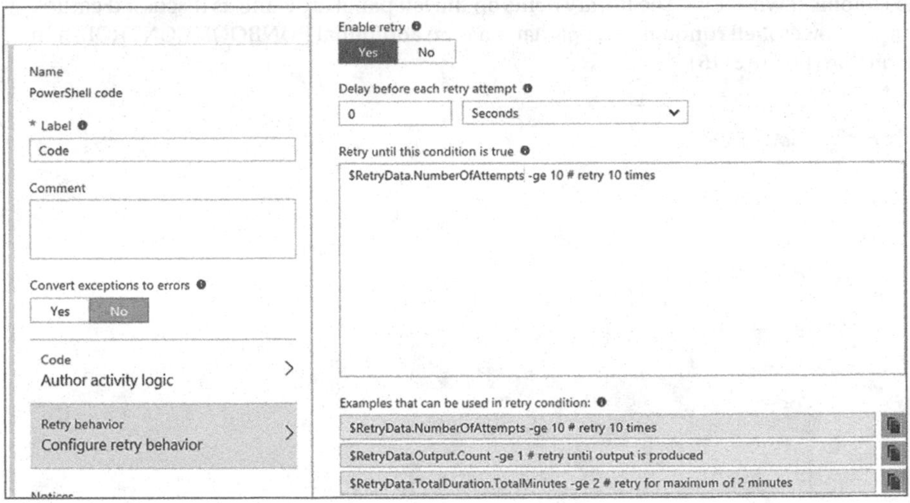

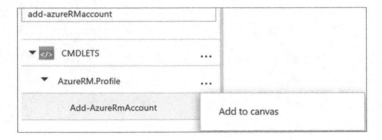

Figure 3-17. *Retry logic*

To start creating your Graphical runbooks from the edit panel, click the corresponding cmdlet and choose Add to Canvas. Alternately, you can search for a command and add it to the canvas (Figure 3-18).

Figure 3-18. *Searching for and adding a command to the canvas*

After adding the command, double-click the command in the canvas to configure its parameters (Figure 3-19).

Figure 3-19. Configuring parameters of the command

Parameter options are displayed, and you can choose one of those parameters based on the workflow logic that you want to implement. Based on the chosen parameter set, you can configure the individual parameters further (Figure 3-20).

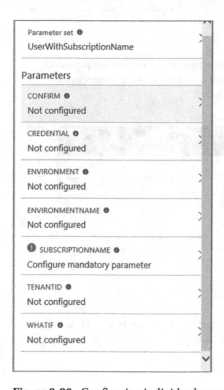

Figure 3-20. Configuring individual parameters

The mandatory parameters are marked in red. You can select from a list of Data Source drop-down options to configure the parameter values (Figure 3-21).

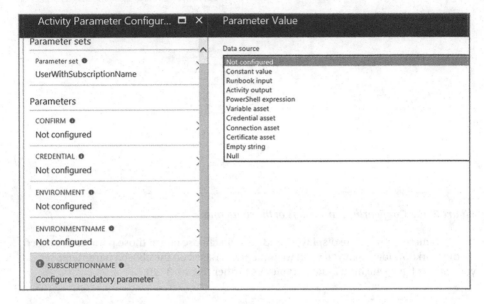

Figure 3-21. *Selecting a data source*

Based on the data source selected, further reconfiguration options are provided. For example, if the variable asset is selected, a list of available variable assets in the subscription is presented to choose from (Figure 3-22).

Figure 3-22. *Variable asset list*

You can configure optional additional parameters such as -Verbose: $true (Figure 3-23).

Name
Add-AzureRmAccount

* Label ❶

Add-AzureRmAccount

Comment

Convert exceptions to errors ❶

Yes   No

Parameters
Configure parameters   ›

Optional additional parameters
Configure parameters   ›

Additional Parameters ❶

Figure 3-23. *Configuring additional parameters*

Based on your workflow logic, you can select the next cmdlet and link them together. To link one activity to another, hover over the activity in the canvas until a small circle appears at the bottom (Figure 3-24).

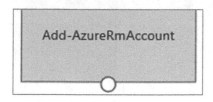

Figure 3-24. *Linking commands*

Click and drag to the next activity box to create the link (Figure 3-25).

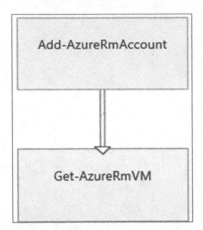

Figure 3-25. *Clicking and dragging to link activity*

Double-click the link to get further configuration options (Figure 3-26).

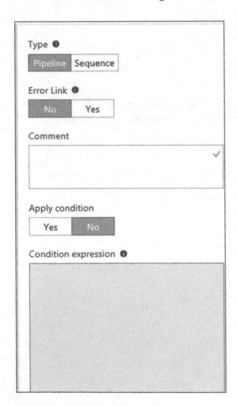

Figure 3-26. *Linking configuration options*

The link type can be Pipeline or Sequence. If Pipeline is used, the destination activity is executed only if the source activity produces an output, which will always be an individual object. The number of times the destination activity is executed depends on the number of such outputs from the source activity. Sequence links, on the other hand, always run once and receive output from the source activity as an array of objects.

Pipeline is selected by default. The destination activity, which is Get-AzureRmVM, will be executed if the source activity (Add-AzureRMAccount) is completed successfully. Depending on the source activity output, the destination activity is executed once for every object output from the source activity. If Sequence is selected, the destination activity runs one time when the source activity execution is completed.

Error Link is by default set to No. You can toggle it to Yes if you want the destination activity to be executed if the source activity emits an error.

You can configure the input and output of the runbook from the edit panel of the runbook. Click Input and Output ➤ Add Input (Figure 3-27).

Figure 3-27. Input and output configuration

The name, type, and default values can be further configured (Figure 3-28).

Figure 3-28. Input parameter

The parameter will be listed as the Data Source when you configure parameters for your activity (Figure 3-29).

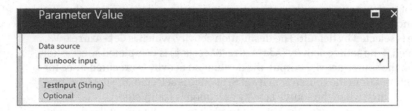

Figure 3-29. *Parameter listed as the data source*

Similarly, you can define the output type as well, which will be used as a data source for parameters. Alternately, for any destination activity, the output of source activity can be provided as an input data source (Figure 3-30).

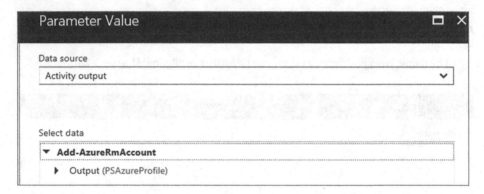

Figure 3-30. *Output as the data source*

After configuring the runbook, you can test it from the Test pane. The last step is to publish the runbook so that it is available in the Automation account (Figure 3-31).

Figure 3-31. *Publishing the runbook*

Now, let's look at a runbook from the Runbook Gallery to put together all the concepts that we've discussed (Figure 3-32).

Stop Azure V2 VMs

Graphical Runbook

This Graphical PowerShell runbook connects to Azure using an Automation Run As account and stops all V2 VMs in an Azure subscription or in a resource group or a single named V2 VM. You can attach a recurring schedule to this runbook to run it at a specific time.

Tags: Azure Virtual Machines, Stop VM, GraphicalPS

Figure 3-32. *Sample runbook*

This runbook stops ARM VMs based on the inputs provided (Figure 3-33). The entire workflow is depicted in the edit pane in an easy-to-understand diagram.

Figure 3-33. *Graphical runbook edit pane*

In the first step, a runbook input parameter is used to retrieve the
AzureRunAsConnection value (Figure 3-34).

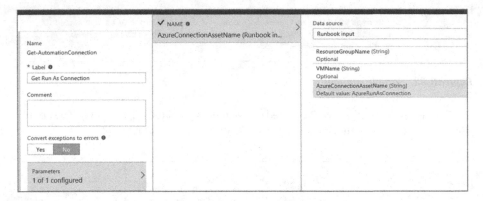

Figure 3-34. *Input parameter to retrieve AzureRunAsConnection*

The next step establishes a connection to the target Azure account (Figure 3-35).

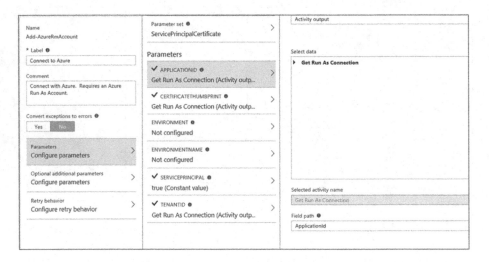

Figure 3-35. *Connecting to the target Azure account*

The activity output of the previous activity is used as one of the input parameters,
and the value to be used is distinguished by the Field path.

A sequence link with conditional logic is created to three target activities (Figure 3-36).

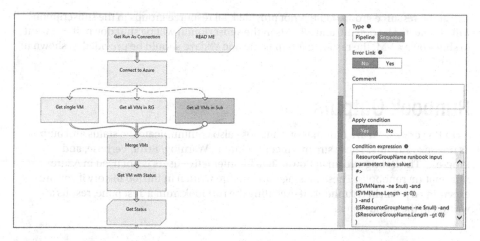

Figure 3-36. *Target activities*

Depending on the input provided during execution and the evaluation of the condition, the workflow will either get a single VM, get all VMs in a resource group, or get all VMs in a subscription. It will then proceed to stop the VMs.

During execution, you need to provide the required parameters. In this case, all the parameters are optional and have default values assigned if not provided during runtime (Figure 3-37).

▶ Start   ■ Stop   ‖ Suspend   ↻ Re

Parameters

RESOURCEGROUPNAME ❶

AzurePPE

Optional, String

VMNAME ❶

Demowebvm1

Optional, String

AZURECONNECTIONASSETNAME ❶

Default will be used

Optional, String, Default:
'AzureRunAsConnection'

Figure 3-37. *Input parameters during execution*

If the resource group name is not provided, all resource groups in the subscription will be selected by default, and all VMs in the subscription will be shut down. If you want to shut down a VM, the resource group name and VMname should be provided as shown in Figure 3-37.

Runbook Outputs

As in PowerShell, Azure Automation runbooks also communicate the status and output as message streams. These streams include Output, Warning, Error, Verbose, and Progress. The Debug stream in PowerShell for interactive users is not used in Azure Automation runbooks. These message streams are written in the job history if you are executing a published runbook. If executing the runbook from a Test pane, results are written in the output pane.

Output Streams

The Write-output command should be used to create output objects. The most common use case occurs when you call a child runbook inline from within a parent runbook. The output objects are passed back to the parent runbook. Alternately, you can use the write-output command from within a function, and the output objects will be passed back to the runbook. The syntax of the command is as follows:

```
Write-Output
    [-InputObject] <PSObject[]>
    [-NoEnumerate]
    [<CommonParameters>]
```

The output type can be declared as an OutPutType attribute. The output type can be integer, string, array, and so forth. For example:

```
[OutputType([string])]
```

Declaration of the output type helps defining the runbook logic, because it gives an indication of the expected output.

Sample code snippets for PowerShell and PowerShell-based runbooks are shown here:

```
Write-output -InputObject $Outputobject
$Outputobject
Write-output " Sample output"
```

For Graphical runbooks, the Input and Output menu (Figure 3-38) can be used to declare the runbook output type.

Figure 3-38.   Declaring the output type in the runbook

Message Streams

Message streams are used to provide warnings, errors, and verbose messages to the user.

Warning and error messages can be invoked by using the `write-error` and `write-warning` cmdlets, respectively. Here is a sample code snippet for error and warning messages that can be used in a runbook:

```
Write-Warning -Message " Warning message"
Write-Warning -Message "Error message"
```

Verbose messages help with debugging the runbook. These messages can be enabled, if required, from the Runbook settings in the Azure portal (Figure 3-39).

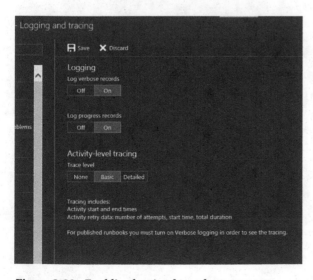

Figure 3-39.   Enabling logging for verbose messages

Summary

This chapter covered the various runbook types possible in Azure. The chapter also provided a walk-through of runbook creation and customization as well as the output streams of a runbook. We also covered a couple of use cases related to the different runbook types.

■ Additional Resources

https://docs.microsoft.com/en-us/azure/automation/automation-troubleshooting-automation-errors

https://docs.microsoft.com/en-us/azure/automation/automation-runbook-output-and-messages

https://docs.microsoft.com/en-us/azure/automation/automation-runbook-types

---

CHAPTER 4

■ ■ ■

Azure Automation DSC

PowerShell DSC is a configuration management solution from Microsoft that can be used across both Windows and Linux platforms. It is aligned with the configuration as a code concept, wherein you can define the desired state of your environments as simple text-based configurations and ensure compliance against these configurations. PowerShell DSC is supported in Azure Automation, where you can upload your DSC configurations, compile them, and apply them to DSC nodes. This chapter covers the components of PowerShell DSC; you'll learn how to create and apply DSC configurations and how the whole workflow can be done again via Azure Automation DSC.

PowerShell DSC

PowerShell DSC works based on the concept of configuration, resources, and the DSC engine, which is the local configuration manager.

Configuration

The configuration defines the framework of DSC, which includes the variables to be used, the target nodes, and the resources for configuring those target nodes. DSC uses PowerShell syntax and starts with the configuration keyword. Sample configuration is given here:

```
Configuration TestConfiguration {

    Node localhost{
        WindowsFeature requiredfeature1 {
            Ensure = "Present"
            Name =  "Web-Server"
        }
        Service requiredservice1 {
            Name = "W3SVC"
            StartupType = 'Automatic'
            State = 'Running'

        }
    }
}
```

© Shijimol Ambi Karthikeyan 2017   87
S. Ambi Karthikeyan, *Azure Automation Using the ARM Model*,
https://doi.org/10.1007/978-1-4842-3219-4_4

This is a basic configuration that, when applied against nodes, ensures that the Web-Server feature is present in the target node. It will also ensure that the World Wide Web Publishing service is started. The target node here is localhost. You can also input the hostname as a parameter by using a param block before the Node block. The configuration can be updated as follows:

```
Configuration TestConfiguration {
param(
        [string[]]$ComputerName="WebVM1"
    )

    Node $ComputerName {
        WindowsFeature requiredfeature1 {
            Ensure = "Present"
            Name =  "Web-Server"
        }
        Service requiredservice1 {
            Name = "W3SVC"
            StartupType = 'Automatic'
            State = 'Running'

        }
    }
}
```

The configuration files can be saved as a .ps1 file and compiled as a PowerShell function to create a Management Object Format (MOF) file. The MOF file contains the desired configuration, which will be applied to the target nodes. Execution of this MOF file is carried out either in the Push or Pull mode by the Local Configuration Manager. We will revisit the process later in this chapter when we discuss the DSC engine.

Resources

Inside each Node block, there can be multiple resource blocks that define the action to be taken on those nodes. In the preceding example, in each target node, DSC will ensure that the Web-Server feature is installed. A set of built-in resources can be used in DSC configurations, or you can create your own custom resources.

The following are some of the important built-in resources available in DSC:

WindowsFeature: Installs a Windows feature and ensures that the feature is present in the target node

WindowsProcess: Ensures that a given process is started and present in the target node

Archive: Used to unpack a zip file to a specified destination path

User: Creates and manages local user accounts

Group: Creates and manages local groups

Log: Logs messages in DSC Analytics log during execution

Package: Used to install/uninstall packages on the target node

Registry: Manages Registry keys

Script: Executes PowerShell scripts

Service: Manages services

File: Used for file and folder management

Environment: Used for managing system environment variables

In addition to these main resources, other built-in resources are available for functionalities defining dependencies, enabling optional features, installing package .cab files, and more. For example, these resources include but are not limited to WaitforAllResource, WaitforAnyResource, WindowsFeatureSet, and WindowsOptionalFeatureSet. We will not go into extensive detail about the resources in this chapter; instead we'll focus on a use-case perspective.

The command Get-DSCResource can be used with the -syntax parameter to get the syntax of the built-in resources, and you can use that as a reference to create the resource (Figure 4-1).

```
PS C:\WINDOWS\system32> Get-DSCResource WindowsFeature -syntax
WindowsFeature [String] #ResourceName
{
    Name = [string]
    [Credential = [PSCredential]]
    [DependsOn = [string[]]]
    [Ensure = [string]{ Absent | Present }]
    [IncludeAllSubFeature = [bool]]
    [LogPath = [string]]
    [PsDscRunAsCredential = [PSCredential]]
    [Source = [string]]
}

PS C:\WINDOWS\system32> Get-DSCResource WindowsProcess -syntax
WindowsProcess [String] #ResourceName
{
    Arguments = [string]
    Path = [string]
    [Credential = [PSCredential]]
    [DependsOn = [string[]]]
    [Ensure = [string]{ Absent | Present }]
    [PsDscRunAsCredential = [PSCredential]]
    [StandardErrorPath = [string]]
    [StandardInputPath = [string]]
    [StandardOutputPath = [string]]
    [WorkingDirectory = [string]]
}

PS C:\WINDOWS\system32> Get-DSCResource archive -syntax
Archive [String] #ResourceName
{
    Destination = [string]
    Path = [string]
    [Checksum = [string]{ CreatedDate | ModifiedDate | SHA-1 | SHA-256 | SHA-512 }]
    [Credential = [PSCredential]]
    [DependsOn = [string[]]]
    [Ensure = [string]{ Absent | Present }]
    [Force = [bool]]
    [PsDscRunAsCredential = [PSCredential]]
    [Validate = [bool]]
}
```

Figure 4-1. *Get-DSCRecource command syntax*

Now let's look at few sample resource blocks using some of the built-in resources. You have already seen an example of the WindowsFeature and Service resources in the previous section. Let's revisit the example so you can understand what that code will accomplish:

```
WindowsFeature requiredfeature1 {
        Ensure = "Present"
        Name =  "Web-Server"
    }
    Service requiredservice1 {
        Name = "W3SVC"
        StartupType = 'Automatic'
        State = 'Running'
    }
```

The WindowsFeature resource will ensure that the Web-Server feature is installed on the target node. The Service feature, on the other hand, ensures that the World Wide Web publishing service is set to Automatic and is in the running state. Note that the Name used here is not same as the display name of the feature/service. You can get the name of the feature and service by using the Get-WindowsFeature and Get-Service cmdlets, respectively.

Here's another example:

```
File Websitenew {
        Ensure = 'Present'
        SourcePath = 'c:\websitecontent\index.html'
        DestinationPath = 'c:\inetpub\wwwroot'
    }
```

This example uses the built-in resource file, and copies the file from the source c:\websitecontent\index.html to the destination c:\inetpub\wwwroot. The use case here is copying a custom index.html file to the inetpub root.

Consider this example:

```
Archive TestArchive {
    Ensure = 'Present'
    Path = 'C:\Archivetest\Test.zip'
    Destination = 'c:\Archivetest\testfolder'
}
```

Here, the built-in resource archive is used. The contents of the zip file Test.zip will be extracted to the Destination path.

Now let's consider a use case of a JDK installation. The following sample code shows how to install the .exe file by using the Package resource and then set the JAVA_HOME environment variable by using the Environment resource:

```
Package JavaInstall{
        Ensure      = 'Present'
        Path        = 'C:\test\jdk-8u131-windows-x64.exe'
        Name        = 'Java 8 Update 131 (64-bit)'
        ProductId   = ''
        Arguments = '/s STATIC=1 WEB_JAVA=0'
    }
Environment Javahome{
        Ensure = 'Present'
        Name = 'JAVA_HOME'
        Value = 'C:\Program Files\Java\jdk1.8.0_131'
    }
```

This can be useful when you want to perform a hands-free installation of JDK using DSC. The .exe file is available at the path C:\test\jdk-8u131-windows-x64.exe. You need to specify the name, product ID if known (it will work even if we leave it blank for JDK), and any arguments that you want to pass during installation. Here we are passing the arguments of a silent installation of JDK.

DSC Engine (Local Configuration Manager)

The Local Configuration Manager, or LCM, is responsible for applying the configuration on the target nodes and maintaining the *as is* state, which is the highlight of DSC. The LCM manages Pull and Push modes as well as partial configurations. DSC can work in either a Pull mode or Push mode architecture.

DSC Push Mode

The Push mode is the manual approach of applying a DSC configuration. The configurations are pushed to the target nodes by an administrator using the Start-DSCConfiguration cmdlet. You can point to the MOF file to be used by using the -Path parameter. The first step is to compile the configurations stored as .ps1 files as PowerShell functions. For example, if the PowerShell script name is example.ps1, you can compile it from a PowerShell prompt as shown in Figure 4-2.

```
PS C:\DSCsamples> .\Example.ps1
PS C:\DSCsamples> example


    Directory: C:\DSCsamples\Example


Mode                LastWriteTime         Length Name
----                -------------         ------ ----
-a----         7/6/2017   12:41 PM           2566 localhost.mof
```

Figure 4-2. Compiling a DSC configuration

You can see that it creates a folder of the same name with a MOF file inside it (Figure 4-3).

Figure 4-3. *Folder with MOF file*

It is this MOF file that will be applied by using the `Start-DSCConfiguration` command in Push mode as follows. You can use the `-wait` or `-verbose` commands to get details of the operation. The command expects the MOF file to be present in the location from which the command is executed. Alternately, you can point to the folder containing the MOF file by using the `-path` command (Figure 4-4).

```
PS C:\DSCsamples> Start-DscConfiguration -Path .\Example -wait -Verbose
VERBOSE: Perform operation 'Invoke CimMethod' with following parameters, ''methodName' =
SendConfigurationApply,'className' = MSFT_DSCLocalConfigurationManager,'namespaceName' =
root/Microsoft/Windows/DesiredStateConfiguration'.
VERBOSE: An LCM method call arrived from computer MININT-S2EIH4C with user sid
S-1-5-21-2146773085-903363285-719344707-2071817.
VERBOSE: [MININT-S2EIH4C]: LCM:  [ Start  Set       ]
VERBOSE: [MININT-S2EIH4C]: LCM:  [ Start  Resource  ]  [[File]MyFile]
VERBOSE: [MININT-S2EIH4C]: LCM:  [ Start  Test      ]  [[File]MyFile]
VERBOSE: [MININT-S2EIH4C]:                              [[File]MyFile] The system cannot find the file specified.
VERBOSE: [MININT-S2EIH4C]:                              [[File]MyFile] The related file/directory is: c:\DSCTestFile.txt.
VERBOSE: [MININT-S2EIH4C]:                              [[File]MyFile]  in 0.0000 seconds.
VERBOSE: [MININT-S2EIH4C]: LCM:  [ End    Test      ]  [[File]MyFile]
VERBOSE: [MININT-S2EIH4C]: LCM:  [ Start  Set       ]  [[File]MyFile]
VERBOSE: [MININT-S2EIH4C]:                              [[File]MyFile] The system cannot find the file specified.
VERBOSE: [MININT-S2EIH4C]:                              [[File]MyFile] The related file/directory is: c:\DSCTestFile.txt.
VERBOSE: [MININT-S2EIH4C]:                              [[File]MyFile]  in 0.0000 seconds.
VERBOSE: [MININT-S2EIH4C]: LCM:  [ End    Set       ]  [[File]MyFile]
VERBOSE: [MININT-S2EIH4C]: LCM:  [ End    Resource  ]  [[File]MyFile]
VERBOSE: [MININT-S2EIH4C]: LCM:  [ End    Set       ]      in  0.1850 seconds.
VERBOSE: Operation 'Invoke CimMethod' complete.
VERBOSE: Time taken for configuration job to complete is 0.347 seconds
PS C:\DSCsamples>
```

Figure 4-4. *Output of Start-DscConfiguration*

By default, the configuration is applied to the machine from which the command is executed. To push the configuration to a remote computer, use the `-computername` parameter. The architecture is depicted in Figure 4-5.

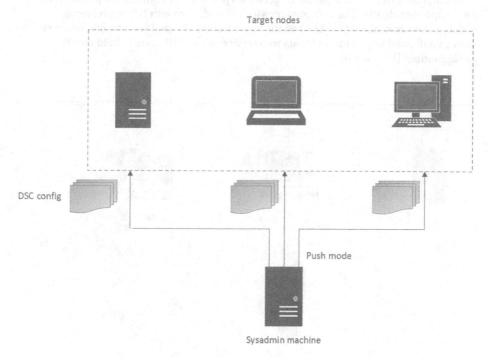

Figure 4-5. DSC Push architecture

No specific setup is required for leveraging the Push mode architecture. However, it is not scalable when we consider large deployments and environment management. A more ideal use case is testing DSC configurations, since that does not require setup of an additional server as a central repository for configurations.

DSC Pull Mode

In Pull mode, as the name indicates, a centralized pull server comes into the picture. In this architecture, the LCM on the target nodes periodically contacts the pull server for compliance checks. The configurations for the nodes are sent by the pull server, which is then executed by the LCM on the target nodes. The pull server could be a web server configured to provide an OData web service or an SMB share to hold the DSC configurations (Figure 4-6).

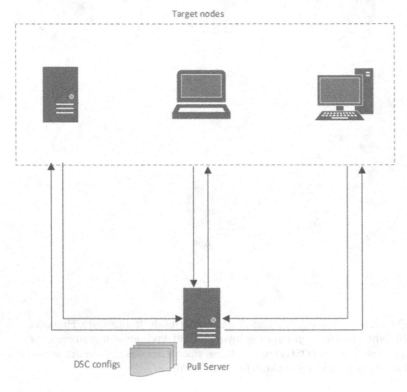

Figure 4-6. *DSC Pull architecture*

Azure Automation DSC uses Pull mode and comes with a built-in pull server. This reduces the complications of setting up an additional pull server to manage clients, thereby reducing operational overhead. In both the Pull and Push models, the engine that finally applies the configuration on the target nodes is the Local Configuration Manager.

Configuration Management Using LCM

LCM is available by default on all machines running PowerShell 4.0 or above. It controls how the configurations are applied and managed depending on the Push/Pull architecture used. You can examine the current configuration of LCM by executing the command Get-DSCLocalConfigurationManager (Figure 4-7).

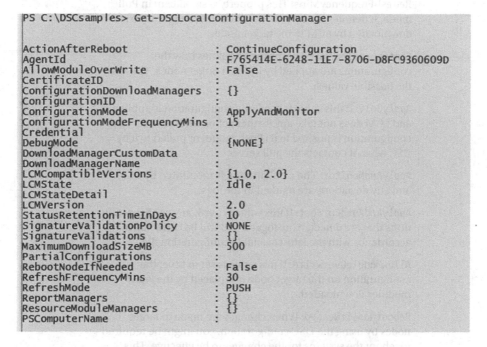

```
PS C:\DSCsamples> Get-DSCLocalConfigurationManager

ActionAfterReboot               : ContinueConfiguration
AgentId                         : F765414E-6248-11E7-8706-D8FC9360609D
AllowModuleOverWrite            : False
CertificateID                   :
ConfigurationDownloadManagers   : {}
ConfigurationID                 :
ConfigurationMode               : ApplyAndMonitor
ConfigurationModeFrequencyMins  : 15
Credential                      :
DebugMode                       : {NONE}
DownloadManagerCustomData       :
DownloadManagerName             :
LCMCompatibleVersions           : {1.0, 2.0}
LCMState                        : Idle
LCMStateDetail                  :
LCMVersion                      : 2.0
StatusRetentionTimeInDays       : 10
SignatureValidationPolicy       : NONE
SignatureValidations            : {}
MaximumDownloadSizeMB           : 500
PartialConfigurations           :
RebootNodeIfNeeded              : False
RefreshFrequencyMins            : 30
RefreshMode                     : PUSH
ReportManagers                  : {}
ResourceModuleManagers          : {}
PSComputerName                  :
```

Figure 4-7. *Get-DSCLocalConfigurationManager command output*

Let's review some of the important properties revealed by this command:

> RefreshMode: In this configuration, the property is set to Push. In a pull server architecture, the value will be set to Pull. It can also be updated as Disabled if you do not want DSC to manage the desired state of your nodes. In one use case, you are using other configuration management tools and want to avoid conflicts.

> ActionAfterReboot: The options available are continueconfiguration and stopconfiguration. This property defines the action to be taken on the target node if it reboots on applying a configuration.

ConfigurationModeFrequencyMins: This property defines the frequency at which the LCM checks for compliance against the latest locally available configuration. This configuration is checked and downloaded based on the value of the RefreshFrequencyMins property. The value is set to 15 minutes by default.

RefreshFrequencyMins: This property is significant in Pull mode. It denotes the interval at which the configuration is downloaded by LCM to the target nodes.

ConfigurationMode: This property defines how the configurations are applied by LCM on target nodes. These are the possible values:

ApplyOnly: If this value is used, the configuration is applied and LCM does not take any further action until another new configuration is pushed to it (Push mode) or pulled to it by DSC when it contacts the pull server.

ApplyAndMonitor: The configuration is monitored by LCM, and any deviations are marked in the logs.

ApplyAndAutoCorrect: If this value is used, any configuration drifts that are detected are logged and will be corrected in accordance with the latest available configuration file.

AllowModuleOverwrite: If this value is set to true, the configuration on the target node is replaced by the latest modules downloaded.

RebootNodeIfNeeded: When changes are made to target nodes by using the DSC configuration, you might be required to reboot the systems for the changes to be effective. This property indicates whether the system should be rebooted after applying the configuration.

Using PowerShell DSC on Premises

The entire process has three phases, regardless of whether the architecture is using a Push or Pull model:

1. *Authoring phase*: The DSC configurations are created as PowerShell functions. The editing can be done in tools such as Notepad or PowerShell ISE.

2. *Staging phase*: The configuration is compiled and converted to MOF files. In a Push architecture, the configuration is pushed to the target nodes. In a Pull architecture, the configuration is stored in the pull server and sent to the target nodes during the refresh interval.

3. *Execution phase*: In this "make it so" phase, LCM applies the compiled MOF files against the target nodes. The MOF files are stored locally in the %system32%\configuration folder (Figure 4-8).

```
C:\Windows\System32\Configuration>dir
 Volume in drive C is OSDisk
 Volume Serial Number is B8B4-3070

 Directory of C:\Windows\System32\Configuration

07/03/2017  06:24 AM                 4,100 backup.mof
07/03/2017  06:24 AM    <DIR>              BuiltinProvCache
07/03/2017  06:24 AM                 4,100 Current.mof
07/07/2017  02:06 AM                   244 DSCEngineCache.mof
06/30/2017  07:02 AM                   502 MetaConfig.mof
07/03/2017  06:24 AM                 3,464 Previous.mof
07/07/2017  02:06 AM                     3 PullRunLog.txt
               6 File(s)         12,413 bytes
               1 Dir(s)  29,958,328,320 bytes free
```

Figure 4-8. *Contents of the %system32%\configuration folder*

The current.mof file will have the latest configuration applied to the node. This is also backed up as backup.mof in the same folder. Whenever a new configuration is applied, the current.mof file is renamed to previous.mof. Another file named pending.mof would be present if execution of any configuration happens to fail. LCM will try to execute the pending.mof file if it is present.

Sample Use Case

Now let's put together what we have discussed so far in a sample use case and apply it to a target node by using a simple DSC configuration.

The DSC configuration file that I am going to use has the following contents:

```
Configuration DSCdemo {

    # Import the module that contains the required DSC resources
    Import-DscResource -ModuleName PsDesiredStateConfiguration

    # This configuration will be applied to the localhost
    Node 'localhost' {

        # The first step is to ensure that the Web-Server feature is
        installed
        WindowsFeature WebServer {
            Ensure = "Present"
            Name =  "Web-Server"
        }
```

97

```
# The File resource is used to copy the index.html file to the
website root folder.
File WebsiteContent {
    Ensure = 'Present'
    SourcePath = 'c:\test\index.html'
    DestinationPath = 'c:\inetpub\wwwroot'
    Force = $true
}
# Here the service resource is being called to keep the World Wide
Web Publishing service running
    Service requiredservice1 {
    Name = 'W3SVC'
    StartupType = 'Automatic'
    State = 'Running'
}

# JDK is being installed using the Package resource. It expects the
exe file to be present in the location 'C:\test'
Package PackageExample{
Ensure     = 'Present'  # You can also set Ensure to "Absent"
Path       = 'C:\test\jdk-8u131-windows-x64.exe'
Name       = 'Java 8 Update 131 (64-bit)'
ProductId  = ''
Arguments = '/s STATIC=1 WEB_JAVA=0'
}
    Environment Javahome{
    Ensure = 'Present'
    Name = 'JAVA_HOME'
    Value = 'C:\Program Files\Java\jdk1.8.0_131'
    }


}
}
```

The comments provide a good explanation of the desired state that will be achieved by applying this configuration. In a nutshell, it will install the Web-Server feature. It copies over an index.html file to the root folder of the server, ensures that the World Wide Web publishing service is started, installs the JDK package, and sets the JAVA_HOME environment variable. Let's save this configuration as DSCdemo.ps1.

In this use case, I am executing the DSC configurations from the PowerShell ISE. The first step is to compile and create the MOF file (Figure 4-9).

```
PS C:\test> .\DSCdemo.ps1

PS C:\test> dscdemo


    Directory: C:\test\DSCdemo


Mode                LastWriteTime         Length Name
----                -------------         ------ ----
-a---          7/7/2017    4:16 AM          4050 localhost.mof
```

Figure 4-9. *Creating the MOF file*

In the next step, we will apply the MOF against the target node by using the start-DSCconfiguration command. In the PowerShell ISE, a progress bar indicates the progress of execution (Figure 4-10).

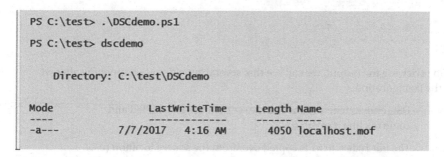

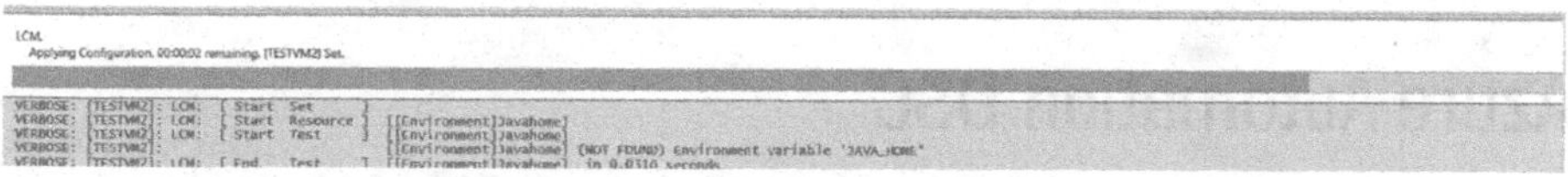

Figure 4-10. *Start-DscConfiguration in progress*

The command used for execution is Start-DscConfiguration -path .\DSCdemo -wait -verbose.

The output is shown in Figure 4-11.

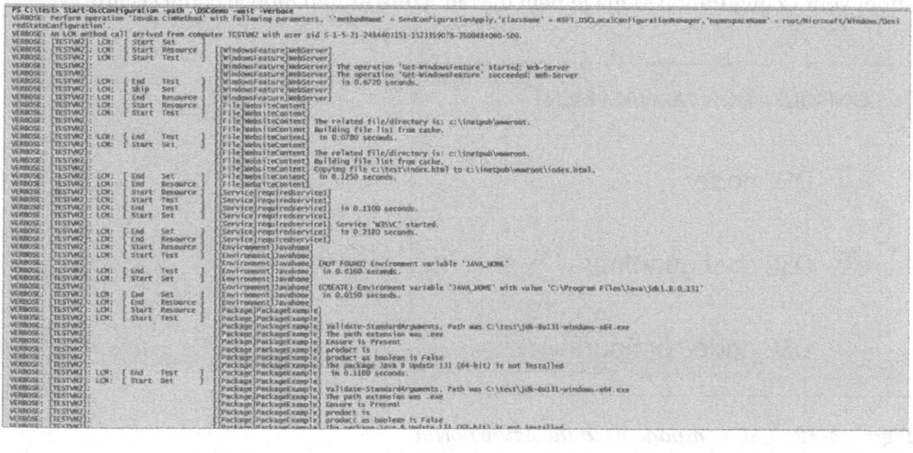

Figure 4-11. *Start-DscConfiguration verbose output*

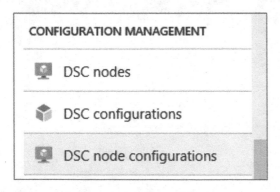

On reviewing the output, we can see that several activities are happening after we apply the configuration:

DSC checks whether the Web-Server feature is installed and confirms that it exists.

The file index.html is copied over from the source location to the inetpub root.

Starts the W3SVC service.

Checks for the environment variable JAVA_HOME. It is not found, and hence DSC creates the environment variable.

Installs the JDK package with the provided parameters.

Azure Automation DSC

Azure Automation DSC is basically PowerShell DSC implemented via the Pull architecture into the Azure Automation suite. The pull server is built in by default. You can upload the DSC configurations to the Azure portal, compile them, and then apply them to target nodes. The target nodes in this case could be Azure VMs, on-premises VMs, or VMs in other platforms such as AWS. Azure Automation DSC provides a truly hybrid and centralized way of managing the configuration of all your systems from the Azure portal GUI.

Let's look at the DSC components from the Azure portal. You can view them listed under your Configuration Management in your Azure Automation account (Figure 4-12).

CONFIGURATION MANAGEMENT

🖥 DSC nodes

◆ DSC configurations

🖥 DSC node configurations

Figure 4-12. *DSC components in the Azure portal*

DSC Configurations

The PowerShell DSC configurations should first be created in an editor such as Notepad or the PowerShell ISE and then uploaded to Azure Automation DSC as a .ps1 file.

1. In your Azure Automation account, select DSC Configuration from the overview panel or from Configuration Management. Click the Add a Configuration option (Figure 4-13).

Figure 4-13. Adding a DSC configuration

Let's select the same demo script that we used earlier in the on-premises example (Figure 4-14).

Figure 4-14. Selecting a script

2. The name of the configuration will be automatically retrieved when you upload a DSC configuration with proper syntax. Click OK to import the configuration. After it's imported, it will be listed under DSC Configurations in the Automation account with Authoring status as Published (Figure 4-15).

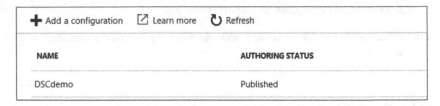

Figure 4-15. *DSC authoring status*

3. When you click the published configuration, it gives you additional options for management (Figure 4-16).

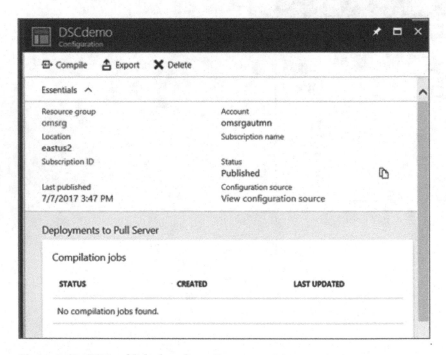

Figure 4-16. *DSC published configuration management*

4. You can compile the configuration from here, delete it, or export it as a .ps1 file from the portal. Click the View Configuration Source option to see the content of the configuration (Figure 4-17).

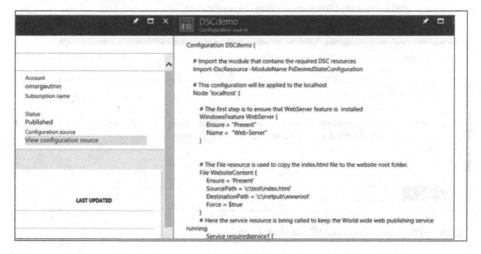

Figure 4-17. *Viewing the DSC source*

■ **Note**　Editing the DSC configuration is not possible from the Azure portal at the time of writing this book.

5. The next step is to compile the configuration. Click Compile. You will get a prompt to confirm the action. After compiling, the configurations will be placed in the built-in DSC pull server in Azure, and any existing configurations with the same name will be replaced. Click the Yes option, and the request will be queued for compilation (Figure 4-18).

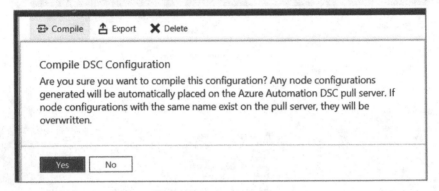

Figure 4-18. *Compiling the DSC configuration*

6. The configuration is then queued for compilation. After the compilation is completed, the pane will show the status (Figure 4-19).

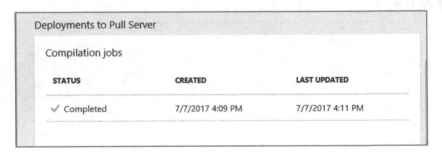

Figure 4-19. *Compilation job status*

7. Information about the node configuration that is available on the pull server after compilation is also displayed (Figure 4-20).

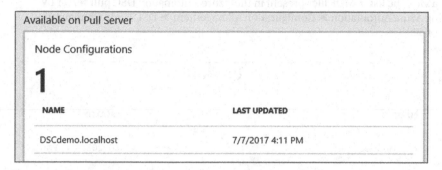

Figure 4-20. Node configuration on the pull server

8. If you click the job compilation status, additional information is displayed, such as errors, warnings, and exceptions. You can click each of the tabs to get additional information (Figure 4-21).

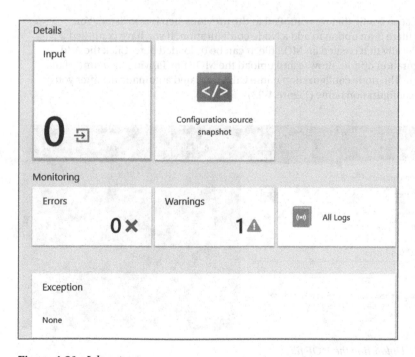

Figure 4-21. Job output

DSC Node Configurations

Node configurations are the MOF files created after compiling the DSC configurations. You can view the list of MOF files present in the Azure Automation DSC pull server by choosing Azure Automation ➤ Configuration Management ➤ DSC Node Configuration (Figure 4-22).

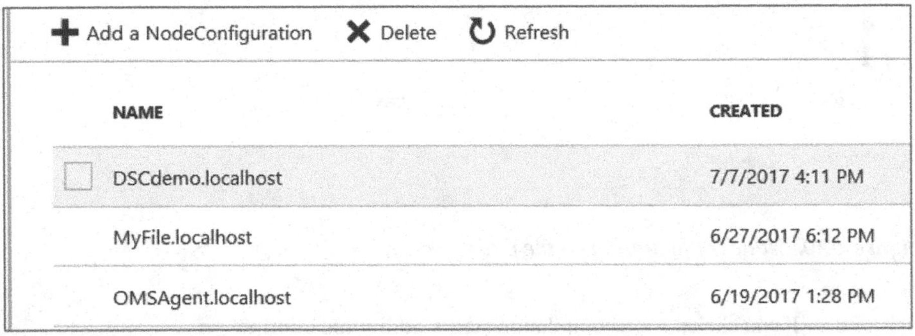

Figure 4-22. *MOF files in the pull server*

The DSCdemo config that we compiled in the previous step is also listed. You can see that there is an option to add a Node configuration. If you have compiled a DSC config locally that created an MOF file, it can be uploaded here. Click the Add a NodeConfiguration option. Browse and upload the MOF file. Provide the name of the configuration. The node configuration name will be created automatically after you provide the configuration name (Figure 4-23).

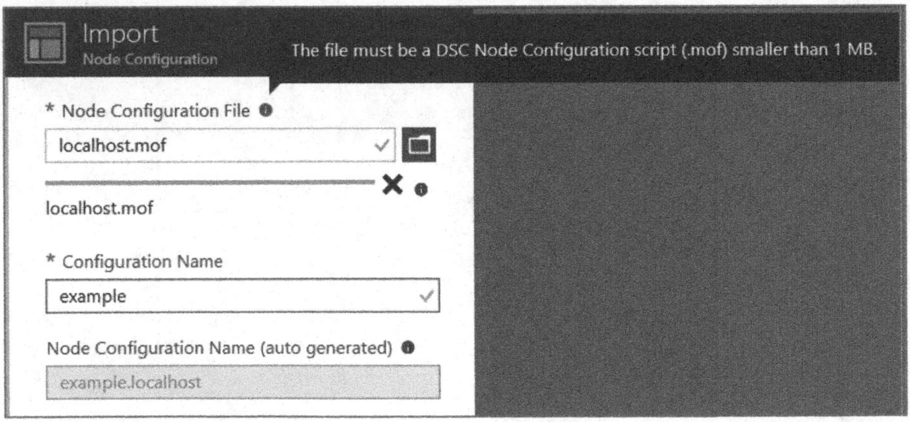

Figure 4-23. *Uploading the MOF file*

The uploaded node configuration is now available in the DSC pull server along with the other node configurations that were compiled from the Azure portal (Figure 4-24).

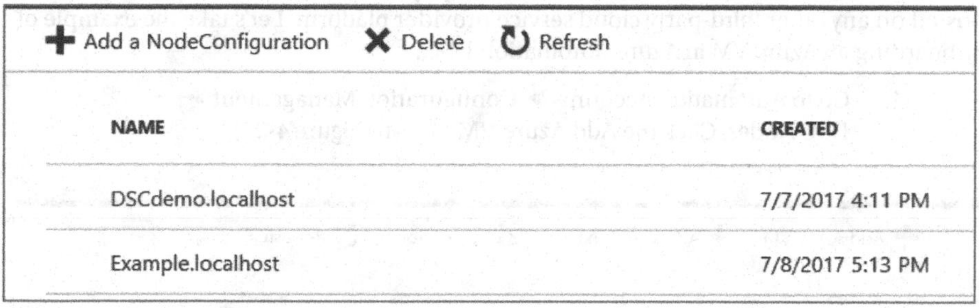

✚ Add a NodeConfiguration ✖ Delete ↻ Refresh	
NAME	**CREATED**
DSCdemo.localhost	7/7/2017 4:11 PM
Example.localhost	7/8/2017 5:13 PM

Figure 4-24. *Uploaded MOF listed in DSC pull server*

This is a good example of flexibility of the Azure Automation platform. Users can choose to compile and create the MOF files directly from the portal, or bring in already compiled configurations that they might be using in their existing infrastructure.

Now that the DSC configuration is imported, compiled, and made available in the Azure Automation DSC pull server, the next step is to apply the configurations against target nodes.

DSC Nodes

Azure Automation DSC can be used to manage Azure VMs (both classic and ARM), VMs in AWS, and Windows and Linux machines (physical and virtual) on-premises or hosted on any other third-party cloud service provider platform. Let's take the example of onboarding an Azure VM in Azure Automation DSC:

1. Go to Automation Accounts ➤ Configuration Management ➤ DSC Nodes. Click the Add Azure VM option (Figure 4-25).

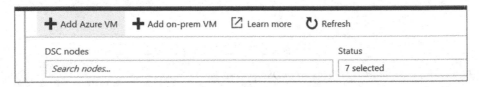

Figure 4-25. *Adding an Azure VM*

2. Select the VM that you want to onboard. Click OK (Figure 4-26).

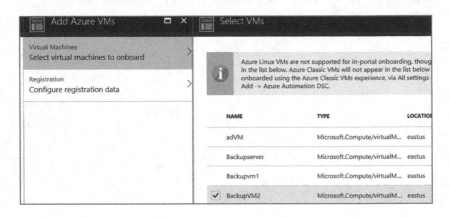

Figure 4-26. *Selecting a VM to be onboarded*

■ **Note** As you can see in the warning message in Figure 4-26, Linux machine VMs, even if they are listed in the portal, cannot be onboarded directly from the portal. It should be done with a registration script. Azure classic VMs should also be onboarded using an alternate process of installing the DSS VM extension separately.

---

3. The next step is configuration of registration data. This is
nothing but the LCM properties to be set on the target node.
The properties of LCM are set, and the node will be registered
with Azure Automation DSC upon completion (Figure 4-27).

Figure 4-27. *Registration data*

The properties being set here are as follows:

The Automation account registration key.

A node configuration to be assigned to the VM. The DSCdemo
configuration that we compiled earlier is selected from the
drop-down list.

Refresh frequency, which is same as the RefreshFrequencyMins
property of the LCM. It is the duration within which LCM
contacts the Azure Automation DSC pull server to get the latest
configurations.

Configuration mode frequency, which is same as the
ConfigurationModeFrequencyMins property of the LCM.
It denotes the interval at which LCM attempts compliance
against the latest configuration downloaded from the Azure
Automation DSC pull server.

Configuration mode, which is the same as the `ConfigurationMode` property of the LCM. You can select from the following values in the drop-down menu: `ApplyAndMonitor`, `ApplyOnly`, or `ApplyAndAutoCorrect`.

Module overwrite is allowed, so that new configurations downloaded from the pull server can overwrite existing modules on the target nodes.

Reboot of the node is allowed if it is required to fully apply the configuration.

Action After Reboot can be either `ContinueConfiguration` or `StopConfiguration`. In this example, we have selected `ContinueConfiguration`.

4. Click OK and then click Create to start the onboarding process. If you click notifications, you can see that the DSC VM extension registration request is being submitted (Figure 4-28).

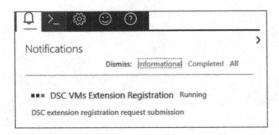

Figure 4-28. *DSC extension registration*

5. If all goes well, you will get a notification that the DSC registration is initiated successfully (Figure 4-29).

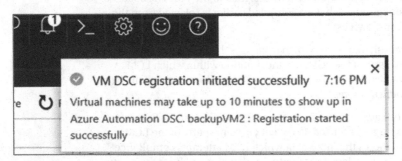

Figure 4-29. *Portal notification*

What happens in the back end is that Azure platform initiates the installation of the DSC extension in the Azure VM and registers it with the Azure Automation DSC service by using the primary registration key.

6. After successful registration, the configuration that we selected during registration (DSCDemo) is applied. You can view the compliance of the node from the portal under DSC Nodes (Figure 4-30).

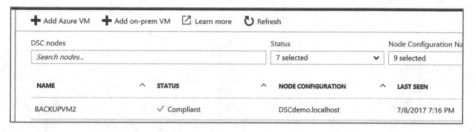

Figure 4-30. *Node compliance status*

7. Click the node to view additional details (Figure 4-31).

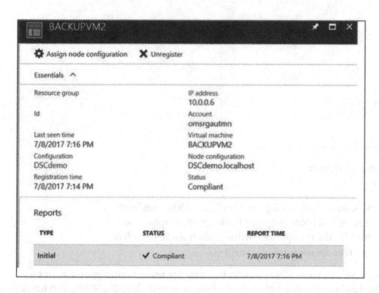

Figure 4-31. *Node additional details*

111

8. You can drill down to further details on the compliance against each resource by clicking the available report (Figure 4-32).

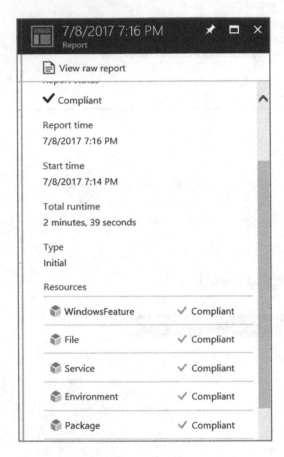

Figure 4-32. *Compliance details*

9. In the DSCDemo sample config, we configured WindowsFeature, File, Service, Environment, and Package resources. The portal provides the compliance information against each of those resources, as shown in Figure 4-32.

If you log in to the target Azure VM, you can see that the node is configured as per the instruction in the DSC config. The Web-Server feature is installed, the W3SVC service is running, the index.html file is copied over to the inetpub root, the Java SDK is installed, and the JAVA_HOME environment variable is set.

Since the configuration mode frequency is set to 15 mins, LCM will ensure compliance against the config every 15 minutes, and the status will be displayed in the portal (Figure 4-33).

⚙ Assign node configuration	✖ Unregister

Essentials ∧

Resource group	IP address 10.0.0.6
Id	Account omsrgautmn
Last seen time 7/8/2017 7:46 PM	Virtual machine BACKUPVM2
Configuration DSCdemo	Node configuration DSCdemo.localhost
Registration time 7/8/2017 7:14 PM	Status Compliant

Reports

TYPE	STATUS	REPORT TIME
Consistency	✔ Compliant	7/8/2017 7:31 PM
Initial	✔ Compliant	7/8/2017 7:16 PM

Figure 4-33. *LCM compliance check*

This comprehensive reporting capability is one of the key highlights of Azure Automation DSC. An administrator will get a view of the compliance status of all target nodes from a single management interface.

Onboarding Linux Machine to Azure Automation DSC

PowerShell DSC can be used to manage Linux machines also because MOF uses open standards compatible with Linux. You can onboard your Linux physical/virtual machines hosted on-premises or in Azure to Azure Automation DSC and manage them through the portal. In this section, we will onboard an Ubuntu 14.04 LTS machine to Azure Automation DSC.

First download the required packages by using the following commands:

```
wget https://github.com/Microsoft/omi/releases/download/v1.1.0-0/omi-
1.1.0.ssl_100.x64.deb
wget https://github.com/Microsoft/PowerShell-DSC-for-Linux/releases/
download/v1.1.1-294/dsc-1.1.1-294.ssl_100.x64.deb
```

Install the packages by using the following command:

```
sudo dpkg -i omi-1.1.0.ssl_100.x64.deb dsc-1.1.1-294.ssl_100.x64.deb
```

The output of a successful installation is shown in Figure 4-34.

```
2017-07-08 20:59:52 (1.64 MB/s) - 'dsc-1.1.1-294.ssl_100.x64.deb' saved [5759228/5759228]

azureuser@ubuntudsc:~$ sudo dpkg -i omi-1.1.0.ssl_100.x64.deb dsc-1.1.1-294.ssl_100.x64.deb
Selecting previously unselected package omi.
(Reading database ... 28885 files and directories currently installed.)
Preparing to unpack omi-1.1.0.ssl_100.x64.deb ...
Creating omiusers group ...
sent invalidate(passwd) request, exiting
sent invalidate(group) request, exiting
sent invalidate(group) request, exiting
Unpacking omi (1.1.0.0) ...
Selecting previously unselected package dsc.
Preparing to unpack dsc-1.1.1-294.ssl_100.x64.deb ...
Checking for ctypes python module...ok!
Unpacking dsc (1.1.1.294) ...
Setting up omi (1.1.0.0) ...
Generating a 2048 bit RSA private key
.........................................................................................
...................................+++
writing new private key to '/etc/opt/omi/ssl/omikey.pem'
-----
Configuring OMI service ...
 * Starting Microsoft OMI Server:
Processing triggers for ureadahead (0.100.0-16) ...
Setting up dsc (1.1.1.294) ...
Installing resource MSFT_nxFileLineResource
Installing resource MSFT_nxFileResource
Installing resource MSFT_nxUserResource
Installing resource MSFT_nxPackageResource
Installing resource MSFT_nxGroupResource
Installing resource MSFT_nxArchiveResource
Installing resource MSFT_nxSshAuthorizedKeysResource
Installing resource MSFT_nxScriptResource
Installing resource MSFT_nxEnvironmentResource
Installing resource MSFT_nxServiceResource
 * Shutting down Microsoft OMI Server:
 * Starting Microsoft OMI Server:
```

Figure 4-34. *DSC package installation output*

The scripts for Linux DSC operations can be found at/opt/microsoft/dsc/Scripts (Figure 4-35).

```
azureuser@ubuntudsc:/opt/microsoft/dsc/Scripts$ ls
2.4x-2.5x  GetDscConfiguration.py              InstallModule.py                          protocol.py             RemoveModule.py
2.6x-2.7x  GetDscLocalConfigurationManager.py  nxDSCLog.py                               RegenerateInitFiles.py  RestoreConfiguration.py
3.x        helperlib.py                        PerformInventory.py                       RegisterHelper.sh       SetDscLocalConfigurationManager.py
client.py  ImportGPGKey.sh                     PerformRequiredConfigurationChecks.py     Register.py             StartDscConfiguration.py
```

Figure 4-35. *DSC scripts*

Let's check the current configuration of LCM by using the GetDscLocalConfigurationManager.py command (Figure 4-36).

```
azureuser@ubuntudsc:/opt/microsoft/dsc/Scripts$ sudo ./GetDscLocalConfigurationManager.py
instance of GetMetaConfiguration
{
    ReturnValue=0
    MetaConfiguration=    instance of MSFT_DSCMetaConfiguration
    {
        ConfigurationModeFrequencyMins=30
        RebootNodeIfNeeded=false
        ConfigurationMode=ApplyAndMonitor
        Credential=NULL
        RefreshMode=PUSH
        CertificateID=NULL
        ConfigurationID=NULL
        DownloadManagerName=NULL
        DownloadManagerCustomData=NULL
        RefreshFrequencyMins=1
        AllowModuleOverwrite=false
        LocalConfigurationManagerState=Busy
        ConfigurationDownloadManagers=NULL
        ResourceModuleManagers=NULL
        ReportManagers=NULL
        PartialConfigurations=NULL
        ActionAfterReboot=NULL
        DebugMode=NULL
        LCMVersion=NULL
        LCMCompatibleVersions=NULL
        LCMState=NULL
        LCMStateDetail=NULL
        StatusRetentionTimeInDays=NULL
        AgentId=F648740C-3F0C-442C-AC4C-8CD9A27EEDC6
        EnableSignatureValidation=NULL
        DisableModuleSignatureValidation=NULL
    }
}
```

Figure 4-36. *Current configuration of LCM*

We can see that by default RefreshMode is set to PUSH. Let's register this machine to Azure Automation DSC. A script is available for this in the scripts folder, which should be executed with the Azure Automation registration key and URL as parameters:

```
sudo ./Register.py <Automation account registration key>
<Automation account registration URL>
```

The registration key and URL can be found in the Azure portal; select Automation
Account ➤ Account Settings ➤ Keys.

On successful execution, you should get the following output (Figure 4-37).

Figure 4-37. *Registration output*

If we check the LCM configuration status now, RefreshMode will be set to Pull, and
the corresponding Azure Automation pull server values should be reflected (Figure 4-38).

```
azureuser@ubuntudsc:/opt/microsoft/dsc/Scripts$ sudo ./GetDscLocalConfigurationManager.py
instance of GetMetaConfiguration
{
    ReturnValue=0
    MetaConfiguration=      instance of MSFT_DSCMetaConfiguration
    {
        ConfigurationModeFrequencyMins=30
        RebootNodeIfNeeded=false
        ConfigurationMode=ApplyAndMonitor
        Credential=NULL
        RefreshMode=Pull
        CertificateID=NULL
        ConfigurationID=NULL
        DownloadManagerName=NULL
        DownloadManagerCustomData=NULL
        RefreshFrequencyMins=30
        AllowModuleOverwrite=false
        LocalConfigurationManagerState=NULL
        ConfigurationDownloadManagers=
        {
            instance of MSFT_WebDownloadManager
            {
                ResourceId=[ConfigurationRepositoryWeb]AzureAutomationDSC
                SourceInfo=C:\OaaS-RegistrationMetaConfig2.ps1::20::9::ConfigurationRepositoryWeb
                [Key] ServerURL=
                CertificateID=NULL
                AllowUnsecureConnection=NULL
                RegistrationKey=
                ConfigurationNames={}
            }
        }
```

Figure 4-38. *RefreshMode value*

The node will be reflected in the Azure portal also under the DSC nodes (Figure 4-39).

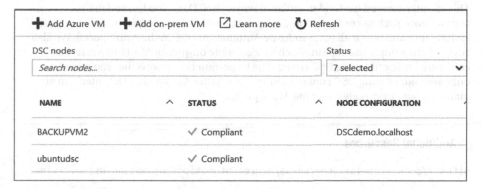

Figure 4-39. *Ubuntu node reflected in the Azure portal*

Note that the node configuration is not present because we haven't applied any DSC configurations yet.

Select the node and click Assign Node Configuration to assign a configuration from the list of compiled configs available in the Azure Automation DSC pull server (Figure 4-40).

Figure 4-40. *Assigning a node configuration*

Azure Automation DSC provides a platform-independent way of managing the desired state of your infrastructure from a centralized portal. Users can create DSC configs, import them to Azure Automation DSC, and ensure compliance against the target workloads, all from the Azure portal. The rich reporting capabilities built into Azure Automation DSC make it easier for administrators to ensure compliance of hybrid environments using this service.

Summary

This chapter covered the fundamentals of PowerShell DSC. You learned the key components, such as configurations, resources, and LCM, as well as the pull and push architecture and how it all maps to Azure Automation DSC in the Azure portal. We also covered one sample use case in which a target node on-premises and in Azure was configured using the same DSC config. The important takeaway is that you can easily onboard your existing DSC configurations to the Azure Automation DSC platform and manage your target nodes from the Azure portal.

■ Additional Resources

https://docs.microsoft.com/en-us/azure/automation/automation-dsc-overview

https://docs.microsoft.com/en-us/azure/automation/automation-dsc-getting-started

https://docs.microsoft.com/en-us/azure/automation/automation-dsc-onboarding

■ ■ ■

## CHAPTER 5

Hybrid Cloud Automation

Azure Automation is a comprehensive solution that can be used to automate administrative tasks in environments hosted in Azure as well as in on-premises datacenters or even third-party cloud service providers. The management of the latter (on-premises, third-party hosting provider, or third-party cloud service providers) is done through Azure Automation Hybrid Runbook Worker. It is also integrated with Operations Management Suite, which takes care of the agent installation, management, and monitoring. This chapter reviews the features of Hybrid Runbook Worker and walks through its usage in Automation scenarios. We will start with a small introduction to Operations Management Suite and how it integrates with Azure Automation.

Operations Management Suite and Azure Automation

Operations Management Suite (OMS) is the management-as-a-service offering hosted in Azure. It is based on services hosted in Azure that cater to specific management tasks. It uses an agent-based architecture and can be used to manage both your on-premises and cloud-hosted infrastructure. OMS has several built-in solutions that can be used for specific management tasks including patch management, threat analysis, health checks on systems such as Active Directory (AD) and Structured Query Language (SQL), to name a couple. It also provides a host of other features such as integration with Power BI and Office 365. The four main components of OMS are as follows:

- Log Analytics: This service monitors and collects logs from various sources, stores it in Azure storage, and then analyzes the data and provides valuable insights on your environment based on the same.

- Automation: This is where Azure Automation fits in. It can be purchased as part of the Operations Management Suite or can be availed as a service from within the Azure portal. However, to use the hybrid worker features for executing Automation tasks on systems hosted on-premises, the OMS workspace is a prerequisite.

© Shijimol Ambi Karthikeyan 2017
S. Ambi Karthikeyan, *Azure Automation Using the ARM Model*,
https://doi.org/10.1007/978-1-4842-3219-4_5

- Azure Backup: This cloud-based backup solution offered by Azure is part of the Operations Management Suite. It can be used for backing up files/folders and applications hosted in systems in Azure and on-premises. It can also be used for taking VM-level backups of Azure VMs.

- Azure Site Recovery: Azure Site Recovery (ASR) is the disaster recovery as a service using Azure, and is part of the Operations Management Suite. The solution offers Azure as a secondary datacenter in case of a disaster recovery (DR) scenario. If customer has an already existing secondary datacenter, ASR can be used for orchestrating the DR between the primary and secondary sites.

Azure Automation is one of the key pillars of OMS; many solutions in OMS integrate with Azure Automation to initiate remediation tasks. For example, you can set an alert for the occurrence of a specific incident and then call a runbook as a remediation step. You should link your Automation account with OMS and call the runbooks associated with that Automation account directly from the OMS workspace. Alternately, you can create webhooks for Automation runbooks and leverage them for OMS alert remediation. An OMS workspace is required if you want to set up Azure hybrid workers to execute Automation runbooks against on-premises target nodes.

Getting Started with Hybrid Runbook Worker

Hybrid Runbook Worker is closely integrated with the OMS workspace and the Automation and Control solutions associated with it. Having an OMS workspace is a prerequisite if you want to use Hybrid Runbook Worker. The Automation and Control solutions should be configured to integrate with the desired Automation account where your runbooks are stored. This Automation account should be in the same region, subscription, and resource group as your Automation account. In addition, there is a dependency on the solution named Automation Hybrid Worker. This solution should be added to the OMS workspace so that the necessary PowerShell modules are downloaded to the target machine.

Hybrid Runbook Worker Architecture

The architecture of an environment integrated with Azure Automation and OMS using Hybrid Runbook Worker is shown in Figure 5-1.

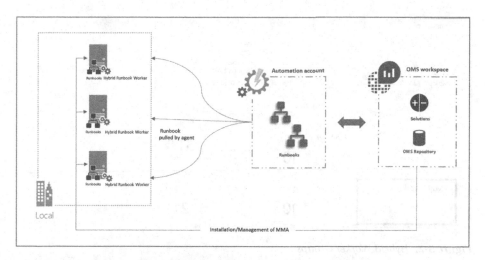

Figure 5-1. *Hybrid Runbook Worker architecture*

The integration of on-premises machines with OMS is done by installing the Microsoft Management Agent (MMA). This agent can be downloaded from the OMS workspace. You will also need the workspace ID and keys for integration. This process is discussed in detail in the next section. The role of OMS is to manage MMA. Once the connection with the OMS workspace is established, you need to configure the Hybrid Runbook Worker so that it is added to the right Hybrid Worker Group in the Automation account. The agent will then contact the Azure Automation account and pull the relevant runbooks and instructions required for executing the commands. Any assets required for executing the runbooks are also retrieved by the agent. All transactions use the Pull model, so there is no inbound firewall requirement. The machine where the agent is installed should have a connection to the Internet over port 443 and a connection to Azure Automation URLs.

Hybrid Runbook Workers are logically grouped as Hybrid Runbook Worker Groups in the Azure portal. To get a list of Hybrid Worker Groups associated with an Automation account, go to Automation Account ➤ Overview ➤ Hybrid Worker Groups (Figure 5-2).

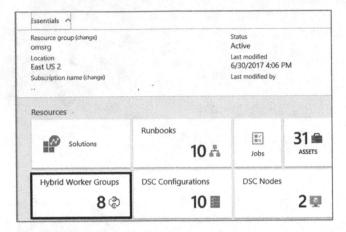

Figure 5-2. Hybrid Worker Groups

Hybrid Worker Groups can have a single worker or multiple workers for high-availability purposes. When you initiate the execution of a runbook, it is the Hybrid Worker Group that you select as a target and not a specific member. This decision is made by the member of the group.

To add a new hybrid worker, click the Hybrid Worker Groups tab from the overview and click Configure. This will provide you with a set of instructions on how to configure a Hybrid Runbook Worker (Figure 5-3).

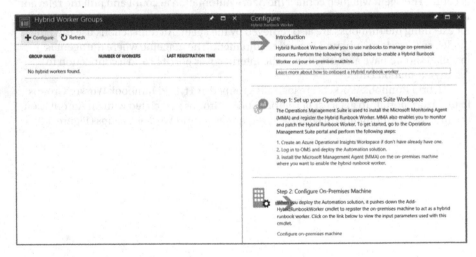

Figure 5-3. Instructions for configuring Hybrid Runbook Worker

Setting Up OMS and Linking It with Azure Automation

You can sign up for OMS at http://microsoft.com/OMS or alternately create a workspace from within your Azure subscription. The step by step process of creating a workspace from your Azure Subscription and linking it with Azure Automation is as follows:

1. To create a workspace from the Azure portal, click New ➤ Data + Analytics ➤ Log Analytics (Figure 5-4).

Figure 5-4. *Selecting Log Analytics*

2. Fill in the details required to create the OMS workspace (Figure 5-5).

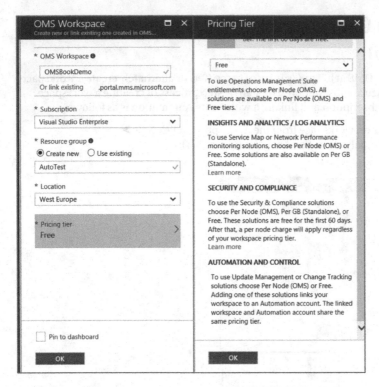

Figure 5-5. *Fill in details to create OMS Workspace*

Specifically, provide the following details:

In the OMS Workspace text box, provide a name for the workspace, or you can link an existing workspace.

Choose the subscription and the Resource Group.

Choose the Location. Note that the Automation account integration with OMS required for Hybrid Runbook Worker is available only in few regions as of writing this book. You can see the latest information on Azure service availability by region at https://azure.microsoft.com/en-in/regions/services/. Check for availability of the Automation and Control service.

The Pricing Tier to be used is either Free, or Per Node if you want to use Automation and Control solutions.

3. From Azure Portal ➤ Log Analytics, select the newly created OMS work space. Click OMS portal to access the newly created workspace (Figure 5-6).

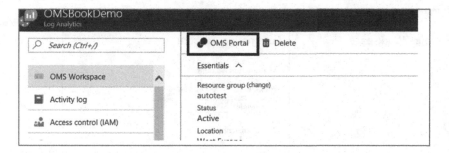

Figure 5-6. New OMS workspace

4. The next step is to add the Automation solution from the OMS workspace so that we can use Hybrid Runbook Worker.

5. Click the OMS home page, click Solutions Gallery, and select Automation and Control ➤ Configure Workspace (Figure 5-7).

Figure 5-7. Configuring the workspace

6. Link your target Automation account with OMS. If an Automation account exists in the same subscription, resource group, and location as your OMS workspace, it will be listed under Use Existing. Otherwise, you can create a new Automation account. In this example, I am going to create a new Automation account. Click OK and then Close (Figure 5-8).

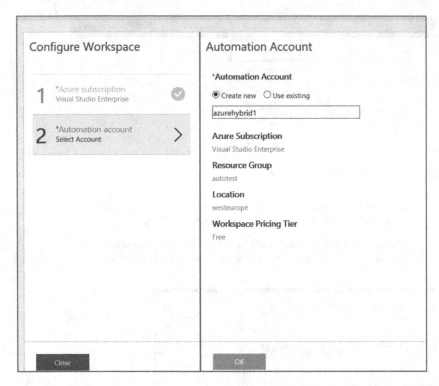

Figure 5-8. *Creating a new automation account*

7. If you check in the Azure portal, you can see that this
Automation account is now created in the same resource
group and location as my OMS workspace (Figure 5-9).

Subscriptions: Visual Studio Enterprise – Don't see a subscription? Switch directories			
Filter by name...		All locations	
3 items			
NAME ∨	TYPE ∨	RESOURCE GROUP ∨	LOCATION ∨
Automationdemo	Automation Account	automationrg	Southeast Asia
azurehybrid1	Automation Account	autotest	West Europe

Figure 5-9. *Created account in the Azure portal*

8. Now that the Automation account and the OMS workspace
are linked, we will add the Automation Hybrid Worker
solution. This will ensure that Hybrid Runbook Worker is
automatically downloaded to the nodes that you onboard to
OMS.

9. From the OMS workspace, go to Solutions Gallery ➤ Select Automation Hybrid Worker ➤ Add (Figure 5-10).

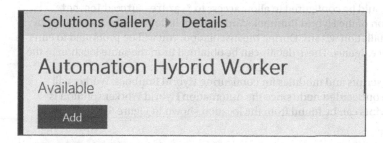

Figure 5-10. *Adding Automation Hybrid Worker*

10. The next step is onboarding of nodes to OMS. This can be done via installation of the Microsoft Monitoring Agent. This agent can be downloaded via OMS Workspace ➤ Settings ➤ Connected Sources ➤ Windows Servers/Linux Servers (Figure 5-11).

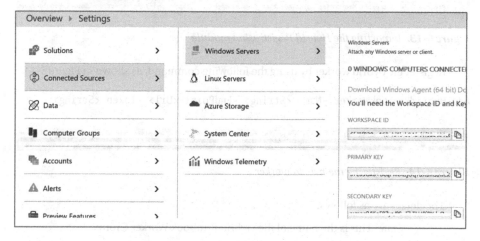

Figure 5-11. *Downloading the OMS agent*

Certain prerequisites should be met before installing Hybrid Runbook Worker:

– Minimum OS required is Windows Server 2012.

– Minimum PowerShell version is 4.0. It is recommended to use PowerShell 5.0.

– The target node should have a minimum specification of two cores and 4 GB RAM.

Hybrid Runbook Worker initiates the connection to the Azure Automation service, so only outbound Internet access over port 443 is required from the target nodes. Also, it should be able to access the Azure Automation URLs. If a proxy server is in the environment, it should be configured to allow access to *.azure-automation.net.

The installation of the Hybrid Runbook Worker agent is done on the target node by using a simple installation wizard. During the installation, you will be prompted to enter the OMS work space details. These details can be obtained from the same location in the OMS portal.

The required scripts and modules for configuring Hybrid Runbook Worker will be available in the onboarded node since the Automation Hybrid Worker solution is enabled. These scripts can be found from the location shown in Figure 5-12.

```
PS C:\Program Files\Microsoft Monitoring Agent\Agent\AzureAutomation> cd 'C:\Program Files\Microsoft Monitoring Agent\Ag
ent\AzureAutomation\7.2.12318.0\HybridRegistration'
```

Figure 5-12. *Hybrid worker script location*

Note that the version at the time of writing this book is 7.2.12318. This could change when new versions are released.

Import the Hybrid Registration module present in this location (Figure 5-13).

```
PS C:\Program Files\Microsoft Monitoring Agent\Agent\AzureAutomation\7.2.12318.0\HybridRegistration> Import-Module Hybri
dRegistration.psd1
```

Figure 5-13. *Importing the Hybrid Registration module*

Register the hybrid worker by using the following command, as shown in Figure 5-14:

```
Add-HybridRunbookWorker –Name <String> -EndPoint <Url> -Token <String>
```

```
PS C:\Program Files\Microsoft Monitoring Agent\Agent\AzureAutomation\7.2.12318.0\HybridRegistration> Add-HybridRunbookWo
rker –Name Hybridtest -EndPoint ███████████████████████████████████████████████████████████████████████
███████████-Token ████████████████████████████████████████████████████████████████████
```

Figure 5-14. *Registering the hybrid worker*

The details are as follows:

- *Name*: This is the name of the Hybrid Runbook Worker Group.

- *Endpoint*: This is the endpoint URL of Azure Automation. The information can be found via Azure Automation ➤ Account Settings ➤ Keys.

- *Token*: This is the primary/secondary key available from the same interface.

Once the registration is completed, the hybrid worker will be listed in the Azure portal under Hybrid Worker Groups (Figure 5-15).

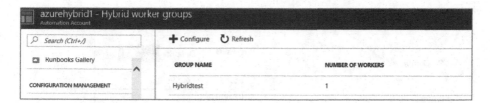

Figure 5-15. *Hybrid worker listed in the Azure portal*

Double-click the Hybrid Worker Group to get additional details of the registered hybrid worker (Figure 5-16).

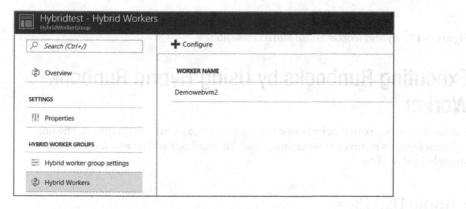

Figure 5-16. *Getting information on hybrid workers*

By default, the Automation runbooks will run under the context of Microsoft Management Agent installed on the target server. However, if you want to use alternate credentials—say, a local admin account to execute the runbooks—a credential asset can be created and assigned to the worker group (Figure 5-17).

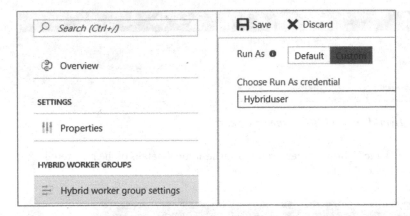

Figure 5-17. *Hybrid worker group Run As credential*

Executing Runbooks by Using Hybrid Runbook Worker

Runbooks can be created or imported using the steps explained in Chapter 3. The only difference occurs during the execution phase. The runbook will be executed against a target hybrid worker.

Sample Use Case

Let's start with a simple workbook that will pull out the list of services with a given startup type provided via the parameters and that is in running status. This workbook could be part of a bigger use case in which the administrator wants to do some additional tasks based on the retrieved data. For the sake of simplicity, we will test this small runbook against the target machine where we had installed a hybrid worker and registered it against an Automation account.

The contents of the runbook for this example are as follows:

```
param(
     # Startup type of the service.
     [Parameter(Mandatory = $true)]
     [string]$StartupType

)

$Servicestatus = Get-WmiObject Win32_Service -ComputerName . |where {($_.
startmode -like "*$StartupType*") -and ($_.state -like "*running*")}|select
DisplayName,Name,StartMode,State|ft -AutoSize

Write-output $Servicestatus
```

When you start the runbook in Azure Automation, change the Run Settings option to Hybrid Worker. For the Choose the Hybrid Worker Group drop-down option, provide the mandatory input parameter and click OK (Figure 5-18).

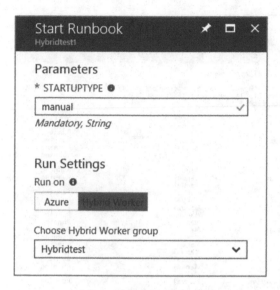

Figure 5-18. *Providing input parameters*

Click Output to view the results. The runbook will pull out the list of manual services in the target machine in running status (Figure 5-19).

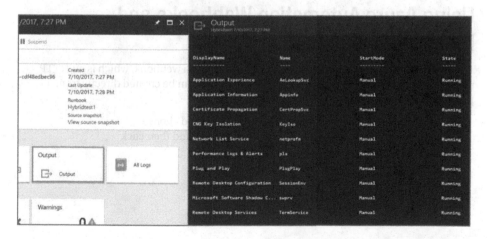

Figure 5-19. *Runbook output*

To verify the outcome, we can run the commands in the runbook directly on the target server (Demowebvm2) where the agent is installed. We can see that the results are the same (Figure 5-20).

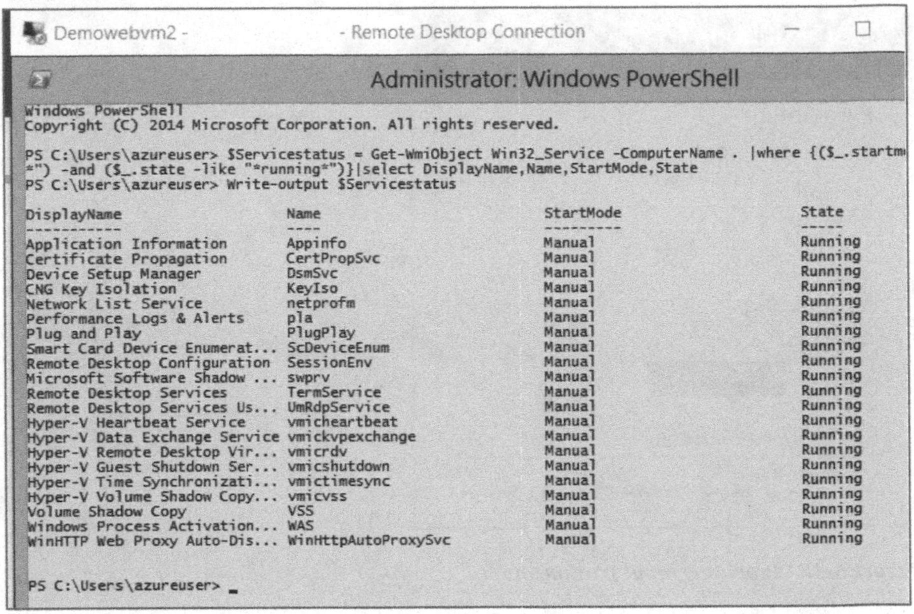

Figure 5-20. *Results from within the VM*

Using Azure Automation Webhooks and Integrating with OMS

Azure Automation can be integrated with OMS by using a webhook, which is an HTTP request that can be used to start a runbook. Webhooks can be created directly from a published runbook as follows.

1. Browse to the Azure Automation account and choose Overview ➤ Runbooks. Select the runbook and then click Webhook (Figure 5-21).

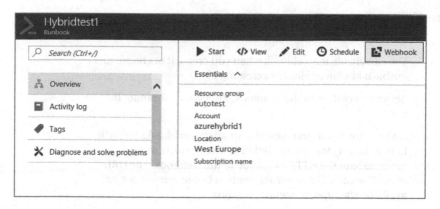

Figure 5-21. *Webhook integration*

2. Provide details of the webhook to be created (Figure 5-22).

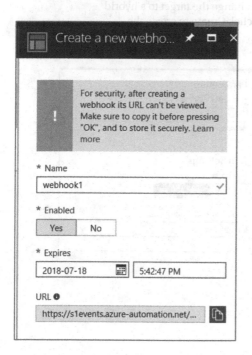

Figure 5-22. *Webhook details*

Specifically, provide the following details:

- Provide a name for the webhook.

- You can enable the webhook when you create it or choose to enable it at a later point after creating it.

- Set an expiry date for the webhook, after which it cannot be used.

- An URL is created automatically for all the webhooks and will have a security token included in it. This security token authenticates the HTTP call made to the webhook. The URL should be copied over during creation because it will not be available after that for security reasons.

3. Configure the Run As option in the next step. Any mandatory input parameters should be defined at this point while creating the webhook. By default, the runbook will be executed on Azure, but you can change the target to a hybrid worker also. Click OK and then click Create to create the webhook (Figure 5-23).

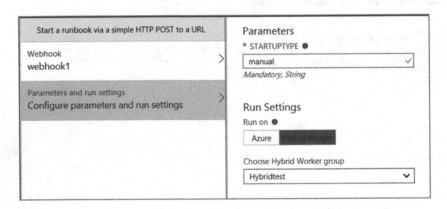

Figure 5-23. *Creating a webhook*

4. Once created, the webhook will be listed when you select the runbook (Figure 5-24).

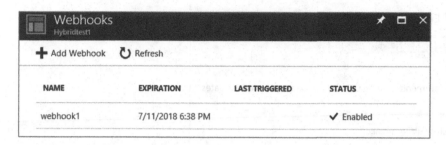

Figure 5-24. *List of webhooks*

5. The parameters, such as the expiry date, can be edited from this view. We can also enable/disable the webhook (Figure 5-25).

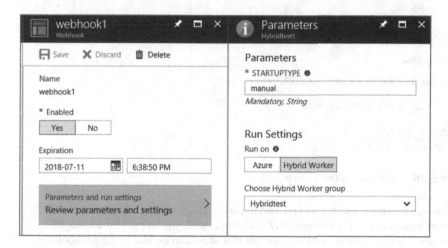

Figure 5-25. *Reviewing the parameters and settings*

Set Up Webhooks in OMS Alerts

From the OMS workspace, click Settings ➤ Alerts to view the list of alerts created. You can edit the alerts. Under the Actions tab, the options for adding the webhook will be listed (Figure 5-26).

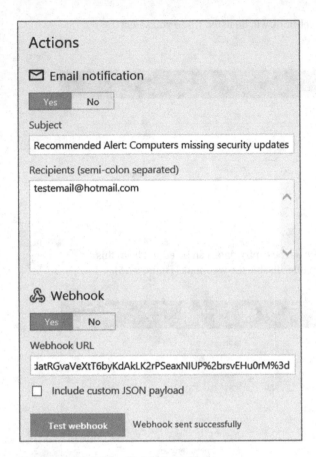

Figure 5-26. Webhooks in OMS alerts

Provide the webhook that was created in the previous section. Click the Test Webhook button to test the functionality. If all works well, you will get the message "Webhook sent successfully." Any parameters that should to be sent to the runbook via the webhook can be included as a JSON file.

Alternately, you have an option to select the runbook from the attached Automation account (Figure 5-27).

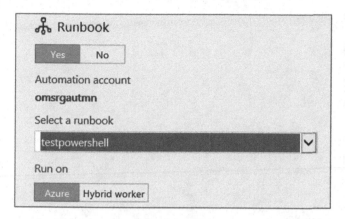

Figure 5-27. *Selecting a runbook*

Once you integrate your Automation account with OMS, all runbooks in the account will be listed in the Select a Runbook drop-down list. This makes it easier for the administrator to choose one of the available runbooks for remediation.

Azure Automation Integration with GitHub Source Control

You can integrate Azure Automation with your repositories in GitHub. You can use this to push or pull the PowerShell runbooks in your Automation account to the GitHub repository.

From the Azure Automation account, select Account Settings ➤ Source Control (Figure 5-28).

Figure 5-28. *Selecting the Source Control option*

Under Choose Source, select GitHub (Figure 5-29).

Figure 5-29. *Choosing GitHub*

■ **Note**   Only GitHub is available as of writing this book. It is expected that Visual Studio Online(TFS) will be available soon.

Authorize the access by providing the GitHub login credentials. If you click Authorize, you will be redirected to the GitHub login page (Figure 5-30).

Figure 5-30. *Selecting Authorize*

After logging in, you need to authorize the account with GitHub (Figure 5-31).

Figure 5-31. *Authorizing Azure Automation*

In the next step, select the repository, branch, and runbook folder path to complete the integration of Source Control with the Automation account.

Once it's integrated, you will be able to check in your runbooks directly from the runbook edit pane into the source control repository (Figure 5-32).

Figure 5-32. *Checking in runbooks*

Summary

This chapter explored how to manage infrastructure hosted outside Azure by using Hybrid Runbook Worker. The features of Hybrid Runbook Worker along with its integration with Operations Management Suite were also explained.

■ Additional Resources

https://docs.microsoft.com/en-us/azure/log-analytics/log-analytics-overview

https://docs.microsoft.com/en-us/azure/site-recovery/site-recovery-overview

https://docs.microsoft.com/en-us/azure/automation/automation-hybrid-runbook-worker

https://docs.microsoft.com/en-us/azure/automation/automation-hrw-run-runbooks

CHAPTER 6

■ ■ ■

Sample Runbooks and Use Cases

Relevance of any technology depends on its capability to handle real-life use cases. Azure Automation is no different. In the previous chapters, we discussed the various facets and components of Azure Automation. Now that the groundwork is done, let's explore sample use cases for the technology.

Operations Automation for Office 365

Some of the common Office 365 administrative tasks can be automated using Azure Automation runbooks. In the first set of use cases, we will explore automation of Office 365 reporting and management using Azure Automation.

Office 365 Reporting

Runbooks will be used to pull out reports from the Azure AD tenant associated with Office 365 accounts. The details can be displayed as output or can be used to create reports that will be e-mailed to the administrator via the SendGrid e-mail relay service.

We will look at two use cases in this section. The first one is a simple runbook to pull out a list of blocked users in an Office 365 tenant. We will use the second runbook to create a password expiry date report for users in each tenant and e-mail it to administrators.

Prerequisites

The MSonline module should be imported to the Azure Automation account before the runbook can be executed. The MSonline module is available in a General availability and Public preview version. Cmdlets in the preview version are not available in the module in the gallery. If you are using the cmdlets from the preview version, the latest module can be downloaded from www.powershellgallery.com/packages/AzureADPreview.

© Shijimol Ambi Karthikeyan 2017
S. Ambi Karthikeyan, *Azure Automation Using the ARM Model*,
https://doi.org/10.1007/978-1-4842-3219-4_6

From the Azure Automation account, choose Modules ➤ Browse Gallery and then search for *MSonline* and import the module (Figure 6-1).

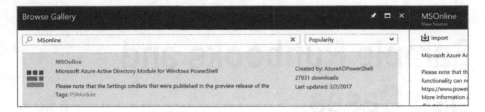

Figure 6-1. *Searching for MSOnline*

If you click the imported module, you can see a list of activities that are basically the PowerShell commands used for the AD tenant management (Figure 6-2).

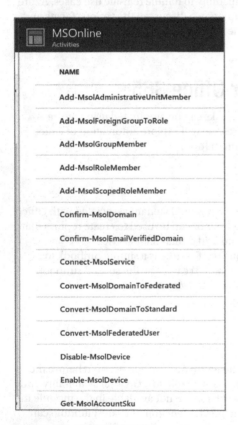

Figure 6-2. *List of activities*

We will use the third-party mail relay service SendGrid in the second use case to send an alert e-mail to administrators.

Search for the SendGrid service from the Azure portal by choosing More Services (Figure 6-3).

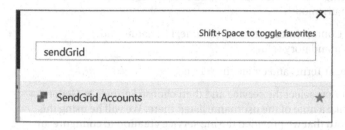

Figure 6-3. Searching for SendGrid

Click the option to create the service (Figure 6-4).

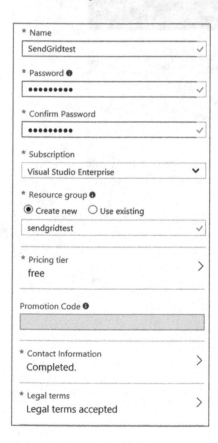

Figure 6-4. Creating the service

Specifically, provide the following details:

Provide the Name and Password, and select the Subscription and Resource Group.

From the Pricing Tier, the free tier should be sufficient for up to 25,000 e-mails/month.

Provide your Contact Information (first name, last name, and e-mail ID) as mandatory values.

Accept the Legal Terms and create the service.

After creating the service, select the service and then choose Settings ➤ General ➤ Configurations and make a note of the username listed there. We will be using this username and the password that we provided during service creation to configure an Automation credential for the SendGrid connection. The SMTP server name will be smtp.sendgrid.net (Figure 6-5).

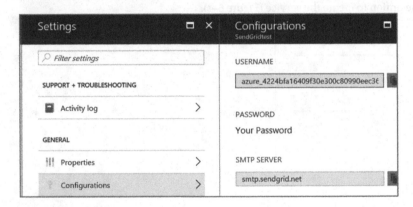

Figure 6-5. *SendGrid configuration details*

The next step is to create the Azure Automation credential asset. We will be creating two assets for this runbook: Office 365 admin credentials and SendGrid login credentials (Figure 6-6).

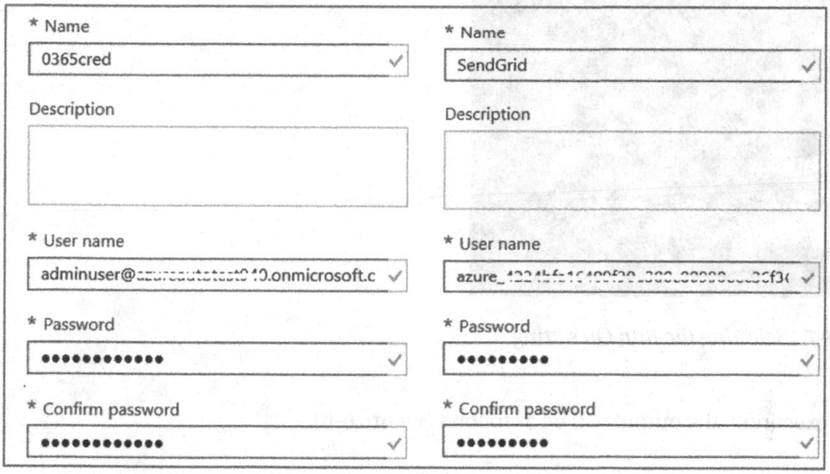

* Name		* Name	
o365cred	✓	SendGrid	✓
Description		Description	
* User name		* User name	
adminuser@azureautotest010.onmicrosoft.c	✓	azure_1234bf616409f20.380.00000...3cf3(	✓
* Password		* Password	
••••••••••••	✓	••••••••	✓
* Confirm password		* Confirm password	
••••••••••••	✓	••••••••	✓

Figure 6-6. *Creating credentials*

Runbook 1

We will start with a simple runbook that will pull out a list of blocked users in Office 365 and display the output:

```
# Connect to Office 365 using the o365 credential object
$credO365 = Get-AutomationPSCredential -Name 'o365cred'
Connect-MsolService -Credential $credO365
# Get list of users
$users = Get-MsolUser -all
# Check for blocked users and display results
$count = 0
 foreach ($user in $users) {
 $displayname = get-msoluser -UserPrincipalname $user.UserPrincipalName

 if ($displayname.BlockCredential)
 {
 $Count = $count + 1
 echo $user.UserPrincipalName 'is blocked' }

 }

 if ($count -eq 0)
 { echo "There are no blocked users"
 }
```

Create a runbook using the preceding content and publish it. Execute the runbook and choose Azure for the Run On option (Figure 6-7).

Figure 6-7. *Selecting the Run On setting*

On execution, the output will be as follows (Figure 6-8).

Figure 6-8. *Viewing the output*

Let's log in to Office 365 Admin portal and verify that the user is blocked (Figure 6-9).

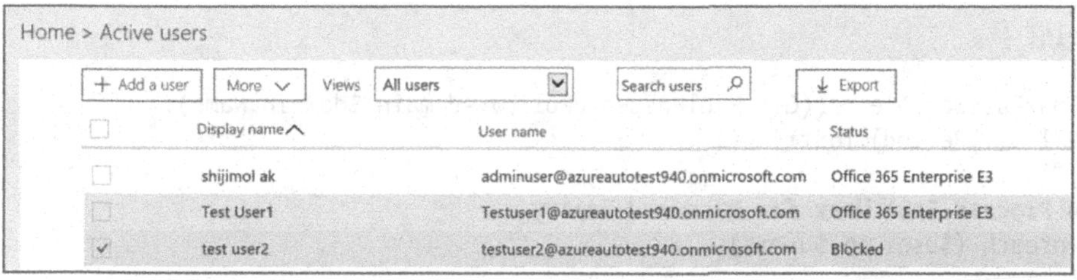

Figure 6-9. Verifying that the user is blocked

Runbook 2

This runbook will pull out a report of the list of users and their password expiry date in a CSV file and send the report as an attachment to the administrator. This can be scheduled as a weekly task by creating a schedule in Azure Automation. The PowerShell script to be used as a runbook is given next. The tasks performed by the runbook are highlighted as comments in the runbook.

```
#Create the CSV, which will be updated with date, name of users, e-mail
address, #days to password expiry, and the password expiry date
$logging = "Enabled"
$logFile = ".\passwordexpirydates.csv"
$date = Get-Date -Format ddMMyyyy
if (($logging) -eq "Enabled")
{
$logfilePath = (Test-Path $logFile)
 if (($logFilePath) -ne "True")
 {
 # Create CSV File and Headers
 New-Item $logfile -ItemType File
 Add-Content $logfile "Date,Name,EmailAddress,DaystoExpire,ExpiresOn"
 }
}
Echo "Logfile created"
# Connect to Office 365 using the o365 credential object
Echo "getting credentials"
$cred = Get-AutomationPSCredential -Name 'o365cred'
Connect-MSolService -credential $cred
Echo "Connected to office365"
# Get Users From MSOL where Passwords Expire
$users = get-msoluser | where { $_.PasswordNeverExpires -eq $false }
$domain = Get-MSOLDomain | where {$_.IsDefault -eq $true }
$temp = (Get-MsolPasswordPolicy -domain $domain.Name).ValidityPeriod
If ($temp -eq $null)
```

147

```
{
$maxPasswordAge = "90"
}
else
{
$maxPasswordAge = ((Get-MsolPasswordPolicy -domain $domain.Name).
ValidityPeriod).ToString()
}
# Process Each User for Password Expiry
foreach ($user in $users)
{
 $Name = $user.DisplayName
$emailaddress = $user.UserPrincipalName
 $passwordSetDate = $user.LastPasswordChangeTimestamp
 $expireson = $passwordsetdate + $maxPasswordAge
 $today = (get-date)
 $daystoexpire = (New-TimeSpan -Start $today -End $Expireson).Days
 if (($logging) -eq "Enabled")
 {
 Add-Content $logfile "$date,$Name,$emailaddress,$daystoExpire,$expireson"
 }
}
Echo " Password expiry report created"
#Get sendgrid Automation credentials
$Sendgridcredential =Get-AutomationPSCredential -Name 'sendgrid'
$SMTPServer = "smtp.sendgrid.net"
$EmailFrom = "adminuser@outlook.com"
$EmailTo = "adminuser@outlook.com"
$Subject = "User Password expiry Report"
$Body = "User Password expiry Report"
#Send email using SendGrid credentials with report as attachment
Send-MailMessage -smtpServer $SMTPServer -Credential $Sendgridcredential
-Usessl -Port 587 -from $EmailFrom -to $EmailTo -subject $Subject -Body
$Body -attachments "passwordexpirydates.csv"
Echo " Password expiry report sent to administrator"
Get-PSSession | Remove-PSSession
```

Once executed, the runbook will give the following output (Figure 6-10).

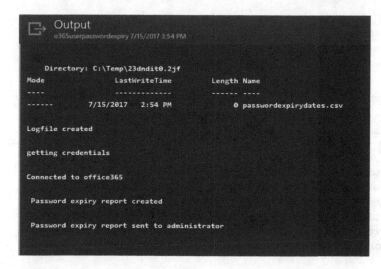

Figure 6-10. Runbook output

The User Password expiry date report will be e-mailed to the administrator via SendGrid (Figure 6-11).

Figure 6-11. Password expiry report

The contents of the report are shown in Figure 6-12.

	A	B	C	D	E
	Date	Name	EmailAddress	DaystoExp	ExpiresOn
	15072017	test user2	testuser2@azureautotest94	88	10/11/2017 17:07
	15072017	Test User1	Testuser1@azureautotest94	87	10/11/2017 9:00

Figure 6-12. *Contents of the report*

Azure Blob Backup

The native backup solution in Azure, Azure Backup, does not support backup of
Azure blob storage at the time of writing this book. In this use case, we will explore an
alternative of leveraging the snapshot feature of Azure Storage to make a backup of Azure
blob storage. This runbook will take a snapshot of the source blob and copy it over to a
different storage account as a backup. A schedule can be created in Azure Automation to
execute this runbook depending on the backup frequency requirements.

Prerequisites

We need the following Azure Automation assets as prerequisites:

> AzureRunAsConection as a connection asset. This will be created
> by default when you create the Automation account. If it is not
> present for any reason, it should be created by providing the
> service principal details for the Automation account (Figure 6-13).

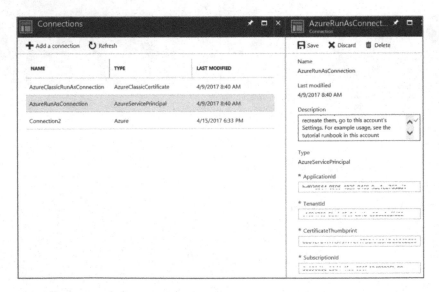

Figure 6-13. *AzureRunAsConnection asset*

An Azure Automation module for storage. You should update this module to the latest version if it is already present (Figure 6-14).

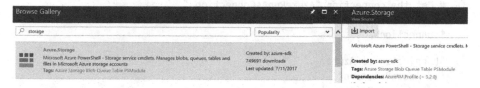

Figure 6-14. *Azure.Storage module*

Runbook

```
#Define the storage account and context.
param(
    # Source Storage account name
    [Parameter(Mandatory = $true)]
    [string]$SourceStorageAccountName,
    # Source Storage account key
    [Parameter(Mandatory = $true)]
    [ValidateNotNullOrEmpty()]
    [string]$SourceStorageAccountKey,
    # Source Storage account container name
    [Parameter(Mandatory = $true)]
    [ValidateNotNullOrEmpty()]
    [string]$SourceContainerName,
    # Source Storage account blob name
    [Parameter(Mandatory = $true)]
    [ValidateNotNullOrEmpty()]
    [string]$SourceBlobName,
    #Destination Storage account name
    [Parameter(Mandatory = $true)]
    [string]$DestinationStorageAccountName,
    #Destination Storage account key
    [Parameter(Mandatory = $true)]
    [ValidateNotNullOrEmpty()]
    [string]$DestinationStorageAccountKey,
    #Destination Storage account container name
    [Parameter(Mandatory = $true)]
    [ValidateNotNullOrEmpty()]
    [string]$DestinationContainerName
```

```
)
$connectionName = "AzureRunAsConnection"
try
{
    # Get the connection "AzureRunAsConnection "
    $servicePrincipalConnection=Get-AutomationConnection -Name
    $connectionName

    "Logging in to Azure..."
    Add-AzureRmAccount `
        -ServicePrincipal `
        -TenantId $servicePrincipalConnection.TenantId `
        -ApplicationId $servicePrincipalConnection.ApplicationId `
        -CertificateThumbprint $servicePrincipalConnection.
         CertificateThumbprint
}
catch {
    if (!$servicePrincipalConnection)
    {
        $ErrorMessage = "Connection $connectionName not found."
        throw $ErrorMessage
    } else{
        Write-Error -Message $_.Exception
        throw $_.Exception
    }
}

$SourceContext = New-AzureStorageContext -StorageAccountName
$SourceStorageAccountName -StorageAccountKey $SourceStorageAccountKey
#Fetch details of the blob.
$blob = Get-AzureStorageBlob -Context $SourceContext -Container
$SourceContainerName -Blob $SourceBlobName
Echo "############Details of blob########"
$blob
Echo "##################################"
#Create snapshot of the blob.
$snap = $blob.ICloudBlob.CreateSnapshot()
Echo "############Details of snapshot########"
$snap
Echo "##################################"
#Fetch time of the snapshot taken
$SnapshotTime = $snap.SnapshotTime
Echo "Snapshot timestamp is $SnapshotTime"
$DestinationContext = New-AzureStorageContext -StorageAccountName
$DestinationStorageAccountName -StorageAccountKey
$DestinationStorageAccountKey
$srcBlobSnapshot = Get-AzureStorageBlob -context $SourceContext -Container
$SourceContainerName |Where-Object {$_.ICloudBlob.IsSnapshot -and $_.Name -eq
$SourceBlobName -and $_.SnapshotTime -ne $null }
```

```
$srcBlobSnapshot | Format-Table -AutoSize
$RestorePoint = $srcBlobSnapshot | where { $_.SnapshotTime -eq $SnapshotTime
}
$snapshot = [Microsoft.WindowsAzure.Storage.Blob.CloudBlob]
$RestorePoint[0].ICloudBlob
#Copy snapshot to backup storage
Start-AzureStorageBlobIncrementalCopy -Context $SourceContext
-CloudBlob $snapshot -DestContex $DestinationContext -DestContainer
$DestinationContainerName
Echo "Snapshot copied"
```

The runbook does the following:

- Create a snapshot of the source blob.

- Then a timestamp of the snapshot is used to identify the latest snapshot from the other existing snapshots.

- The snapshot is copied over to backup storage account by using the Start-AzureStorageBlobIncrementalCopy command, which initiates an incremental copy of the snapshot.

The runbook expects the following inputs to be provided during execution: the source storage, access key, container name, name of the blob to be backed up, destination (backup) storage, access key, and container name (Figure 6-15).

Figure 6-15. *Input parameters*

153

On successful execution, output of the runbook will be as shown in Figure 6-16.

Figure 6-16. *Runbook output*

We can use the Azure Storage explorer tool to view the snapshots being created in the source storage account and then later being copied over to the destination storage. Source blob snapshots are shown in Storage explorer view (Figure 6-17).

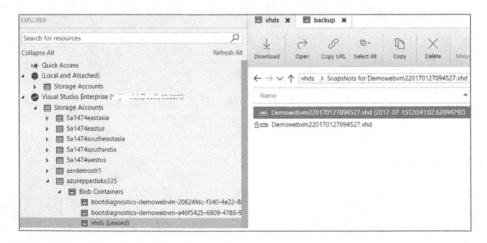

Figure 6-17. *Source blob snapshots*

In Backup storage view, the snapshots are being copied over to a container named *backup* in this storage (Figure 6-18).

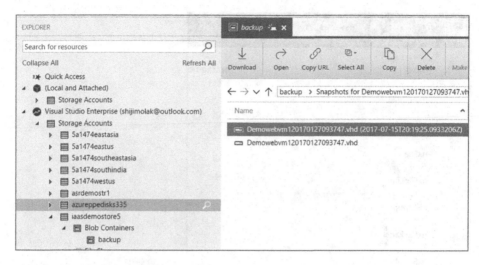

Figure 6-18. *Backup storage view*

Linux Node DSC Configuration Management

In this use case, we will install a package in a Linux node using DSC and then start the corresponding service associated with it. We will install the reverse proxy software nginx using this runbook and start the service.

Prerequisites

The Linux node should be onboarded to the Azure Automation DSC account. The steps were explained in Chapter 4. The next step is to import the nx module into the Automation account that includes the DSC resources for Linux (Figure 6-19).

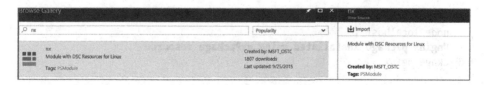

Figure 6-19. *Importing the nx module*

This module comes with built-in resources similar to the resources available for Windows (Figure 6-20).

Figure 6-20. *Activities in the nx module*

We will be using the nxPackage and nXService resources in our runbook, which are used for package management and service management, respectively.

Runbook

```
configuration nginxlinux {

    Import-DscResource -ModuleName nx
    node localhost {
    #nginx package installed using nxPackage resource
nxPackage nginx
{
    Name = "nginx"
    Ensure = "Present"
    PackageManager = "Apt"
}
```

```
#nginx service status checked using nxService resource
nxService nginxservice
        {
            Name = "nginx"
            Controller = "init"
            Enabled = $true
            State = "Running"
        }

}
 }
```

Create the runbook and compile it. Before applying the configuration, we will
tweak the LCM on the target node to make the refresh interval smaller and the change
configuration mode to AplyAndMonitor. Thus we can ensure that the configuration is
pulled from the Azure Automation pull server and applied immediately. Here is the
command to be used:

```
sudo ./Register.py --RegistrationKey <Automation account
registration key>  --ServerURL <Automation account registration
URL> --RefreshFrequencyMins 5 --ConfigurationModeFrequencyMins 5
--ConfigurationMode ApplyAndAutoCorrect
```

Before applying the DSC config, we will check the nginx service status in the target
node. The service will be listed as unrecognized (Figure 6-21).

```
azureuser@ubuntudsc:/opt/microsoft/dsc/Scripts$ service nginx status
nginx: unrecognized service
```

Figure 6-21. *Checking service status*

Select the node from the Azure Automation DSC node list and then choose Assign
Node Configuration. Select the compiled node configuration and click OK. The new
configuration will be applied, and after some time the node status will be shown as
compliant (Figure 6-22).

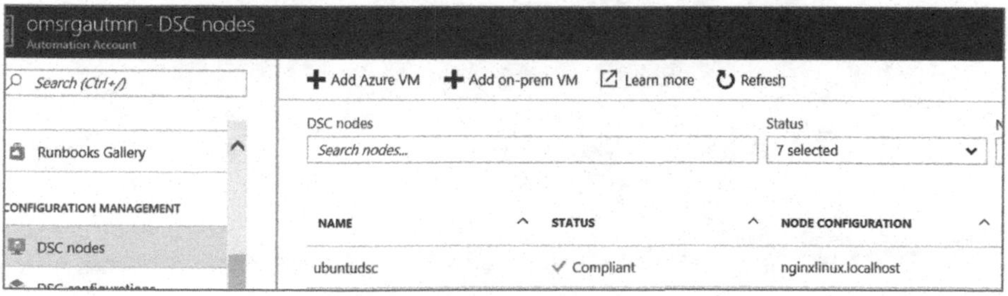

Figure 6-22. *Applying the DSC configuration*

Let's go back to the target node and review the service status (Figure 6-23).

```
azureuser@ubuntudsc:/opt/microsoft/dsc/Scripts$ service nginx status
 * nginx is running
```

Figure 6-23. *Reviewing the service status*

The nginx service will be available at port 80 of the server (Figure 6-24).

Figure 6-24. *Nginx web page*

DSC Composite Resources in Azure Automation

DSC composite resources can be used in Azure Automation in such a way that the configurations can be reused. The composite resources can be imported as modules in Azure Automation. In simple terms, the composite resource is a DSC configuration that can accept input parameters. When we convert them as modules in Azure Automation, they can be imported from another DSC configuration and then the values of parameters can be passed on. The parameters in this context will act as the properties of the DSC composite resource. In this use case, we will create a DSC composite resource, upload it as module in Azure Automation, and finally call this module from another DSC configuration, thereby enabling reusability.

Step 1: Create DSC Composite Resource

There is a specific folder structure to be followed while creating a DSC composite resource that can be uploaded to Azure Automation DSC as a module. The folder structure is shown in Figure 6-25.

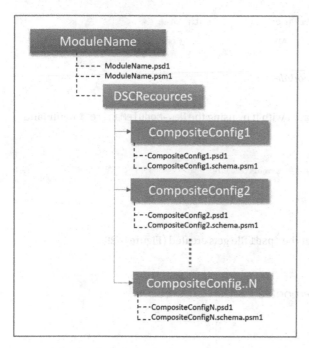

Figure 6-25. *Composite resource folder structure*

Create the root folder with the name of the module that you want to create. It should contain the corresponding `.psm1` module file and the manifest file `.psd1`. There should be a folder named `DSCResources` inside the root folder. The DSC composite resources should be present inside the `DSCResources` folder. These composite resources should have a `.psd1` as well as `.schema.psm1` file. The `.schema.psm1` extension is required to mark it as a composite resource. This file will contain the contents of the DSC configuration, which can be later called as resources by other configurations in Azure Automation DSC.

Let's start by creating the root module folder (Figure 6-26).

```
PS C:\>  $Modulename = "c:\Compositemodule"
PS C:\> mkdir $Modulename


    Directory: C:\

Mode                LastWriteTime         Length Name
----                -------------         ------ ----
d-----         7/17/2017   11:50 AM              Compositemodule
```

Figure 6-26. *Creating the root module*

Create the .psd1 file associated with it by using the New-ModuleManifest command (Figure 6-27).

```
PS C:\> New-ModuleManifest  -RootModule  Compositemodule  -Path "$Modulename\compositemodule.psd1"
PS C:\>
```

Figure 6-27. *Creating the .psd1 file*

In the folder, we can see that the .psd1 file gets created (Figure 6-28).

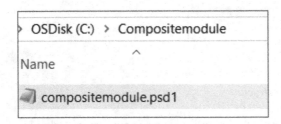

Figure 6-28. *Listing the .psd1 file*

Part of the content of the file is shown in Figure 6-29.

```
compositemodule.psd1 ✕

 1   #
 2   # Module manifest for module 'compositemodule'
 3   #
 4   # Generated by: user1
 5   #
 6   # Generated on: 7/17/2017
 7   #
 8
 9   ⊟@{
10
11   # Script module or binary module file associated with this manifest.
12   RootModule = 'Compositemodule'
13
14   # Version number of this module.
15   ModuleVersion = '1.0'
16
17   # Supported PSEditions
18   # CompatiblePSEditions = @()
19
20   # ID used to uniquely identify this module
21   GUID = '98379e2d-4778-45f5-b02a-1df1392e1cdf'
22
23   # Author of this module
24   Author = 'user1'
25
26   # Company or vendor of this module
27   CompanyName = 'Unknown'
28
29   # Copyright statement for this module
30   Copyright = '(c) 2017 shiak. All rights reserved.'
31
32   # Description of the functionality provided by this module
33   # Description = ''
34
35   # Minimum version of the Windows PowerShell engine required by this module
36   # PowerShellVersion = ''
37
38   # Name of the Windows PowerShell host required by this module
39   # PowerShellHostName = ''
40
41   # Minimum version of the Windows PowerShell host required by this module
42   # PowerShellHostVersion = ''
```

Figure 6-29. *Contents of the file*

You can see that the manifest contains metadata information, any defined prerequisites, any functions, cmdlets, aliases to be exported, and so forth.

Create a blank .psm1 file in the same folder with any content, which could even be a comment (Figure 6-30).

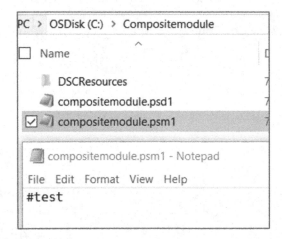

Figure 6-30. *Creating a .psm1 file*

This file is required for uploading the module in Azure Automation.

The next step is to create the DSCResources folder and the composite resource folder inside the root folder (Figure 6-31).

```
PS C:\> mkdir "$Modulename\DSCResources\Composite1"


    Directory: C:\Compositemodule\DSCResources


Mode                LastWriteTime         Length Name
----                -------------         ------ ----
d-----       7/17/2017   12:20 PM                Composite1
```

Figure 6-31. *Creating the DSCResources and composite resource folders*

Create a manifest for the composite resource named Composite1. This time, we will be creating the schema.psm1 file as well, which identifies this as a composite resource (Figure 6-32).

```
PS C:\> New-ModuleManifest  -RootModule  'Composite1.schema.psm1'  -Path "$Modulename\DSCResources\Composite1\composite1.psd1"
PS C:\> Add-Content -Path "$Modulename\DSCResources\Composite1\Composite1.schema.psm1" -Value '
```

Figure 6-32. *Creating the manifest*

The files get created inside the Composite1 folder (Figure 6-33).

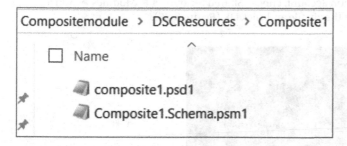

Figure 6-33. List of created files

The contents of the .psd1 file will be similar to the Compositemodule.psd1 file created earlier. In the composite1.schema.psm1 file, add your DSC configuration (Figure 6-34).

```
Composite1.Schema.psm1  X
 1
 2  configuration Composite1 {
 3
 4      File 'filecreate' {
 5          DestinationPath = 'C:\NewFile.txt'
 6          Contents = 'Composite DSC test'
 7          Ensure = 'Present'
 8      }
 9  }
10
```

Figure 6-34. Adding the DSC configuration

We will go with a simple configuration to create a new file and add content to it. Note that the node statement is not present, since this DSC configuration will be used to create a resource that will be called by other configurations.

We have now created all the required files for the module. To create the module, simple zip the root folder to create a compositemodule.zip file and upload it to Azure Automation.

Step 2: Import Module in Azure Automation

From the Azure Automation account, choose Shared Resources ➤ Modules ➤ Add a Module ➤ Browse. Select the zip file and click OK (Figure 6-35).

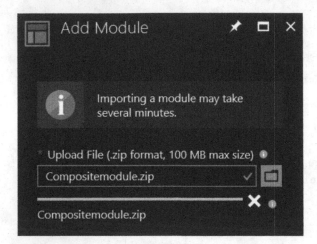

Figure 6-35. Importing the module

You will get a notification that the file is successfully uploaded and the activities are being extracted (Figure 6-36).

Figure 6-36. Extracting activities

If the module is successfully uploaded, you can see the composite resource listed as an activity under the module (Figure 6-37).

Figure 6-37. *Comsposite resource listed as activity*

Step 3: Create DSC Configuration That calls the Uploaded Modules

We will create a basic DSC configuration that calls the resource Composite1 from the uploaded modules. Note that there are no parameters in this resource; however, if your original DSC composite resource expects parameters, it can be passed on at this point from with the DSC configuration.

```
Configuration dsccompositemodtest {

    Import-DscResource -ModuleName PSDesiredStateConfiguration
    Import-DscResource -ModuleName Compositemodule

    Node localhost {
        Composite1 server1 {

        }
    }
}
```

Save the contents as a .ps1 file and upload it to the Azure Automation DSC configuration (Figure 6-38).

Figure 6-38. *Uploading the .ps1 file*

Compile the configuration. If all goes well, the configuration will be successfully compiled (Figure 6-39).

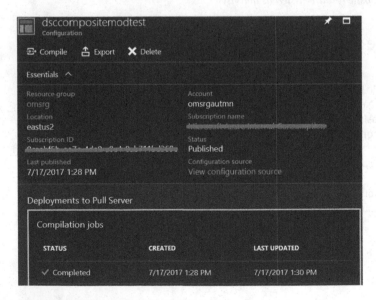

Figure 6-39. *Compiling the configuration*

The next step is to apply this configuration against a target node. Select the node from the Azure Automation account and then choose Configuration Management ➤ DSC Nodes. Click the Assign Node Configuration option and select the newly compiled MOF from the pull server (Figure 6-40).

Figure 6-40. *Assigning the node configuration*

The configuration will be updated when the target node contacts the pull server the next time. Until that time, the status will be shown as pending (Figure 6-41).

Figure 6-41. *Status before the node contacts the pull server*

Once the configuration is updated, the status will be compliant (Figure 6-42).

Figure 6-42. *Status after the configuration is updated*

167

You can double-click the node to get more details about the configuration being applied (Figure 6-43).

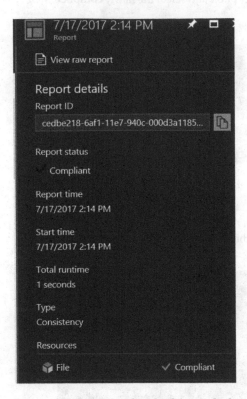

Figure 6-43. Viewing details of the applied configuration

It is interesting to note that the File resource originally defined in the DSC composite resource is being listed here.

As a final step, let's log in to the server and check whether the file is present in the C drive with the contents defined in the DSC configuration (Figure 6-44).

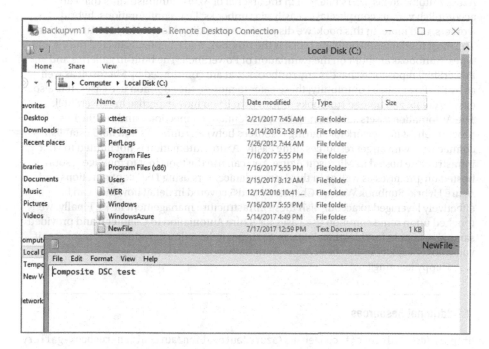

Figure 6-44. *Status in the target server*

The file is present, and we can conclude that the DSC composite configuration is successfully applied via Azure Automation DSC.

Summary

This chapter, the last one in this book, covered different practical use cases of Azure Automation. This includes Office 365 automation and management, Linux machine management, and complex configurations such as DSC composite resources.

Conclusion

Azure Automation is a versatile tool in the arsenal of Azure administrators that can accomplish various complex tasks easily via runbooks, DSC configurations, hybrid workers, and more. In this book, we discussed the building blocks of Azure Automation. The most fundamental building block is the runbook, and Chapter 3 covered the various types. Runbooks are built on the foundation of PowerShell. The built-in galleries and PowerShell repositories have many runbooks that are contributed by Microsoft as well as by the PowerShell community; these cater to most of the common use cases. It is also easy to create and upload runbooks of your own if you have expertise in PowerShell. The Automation assets such as variables, credentials, connections, and certificates prove a robust framework for sharing resources between runbooks and help establish connections with target resources quite easily. Azure Automation is not limited to your infrastructure hosted in Microsoft Azure. You can use the tools in it to manage resources hosted on-premises as well as in third-party datacenters using DSC configurations and Azure Hybrid Runbook Worker. Chapters 4 and 5 covered in detail how they can be effectively leveraged to accomplish these infrastructure management tasks. Finally, we touched upon some common use cases for Azure Automation in Chapter 6 and provided sample runbooks for the same. You can go through the following additional resources if you want to explore more about Azure Automation.

Happy learning!!

■ Additional Resources

https://docs.microsoft.com/en-us/azure/automation/automation-runbook-gallery

https://gallery.technet.microsoft.com/scriptcenter/site/search?f[0].
Type=RootCategory&f[0].Value=WindowsAzure&f[1].Type=SubCategory&f[1].
Value=WindowsAzure_automation&f[1].Text=Automation

https://www.powershellgallery.com/

https://docs.microsoft.com/en-us/powershell/dsc/overview

https://docs.microsoft.com/en-us/powershell/dsc/decisionmaker

https://docs.microsoft.com/en-us/azure/automation/automation-dsc-diagnostics

https://docs.microsoft.com/en-us/azure/automation/automation-azure-vm-alert-integration

https://azure.microsoft.com/en-us/blog/tag/azure-automation/

Index

Get the eBook for only $5!

Why limit yourself?

With most of our titles available in both PDF and ePUB format, you can access your content wherever and however you wish—on your PC, phone, tablet, or reader.

Since you've purchased this print book, we are happy to offer you the eBook for just $5.

To learn more, go to http://www.apress.com/companion or contact support@apress.com.

Apress®